Linguistics in a Colonial World

D0858520

Linguistics in a Colonial World:
A Story of Language, Meaning, and Power

Joseph Errington

Blackwell Publishing

© 2008 by J. Joseph Errington

BLACKWELL PUBLISHING

350 Main Street, Malden, MA 02148-5020, USA
9600 Garsington Road, Oxford OX4 2DQ, UK
550 Swanston Street, Carlton, Victoria 3053, Australia

The right of J. Joseph Errington to be identified as the Author of this
Work has been asserted in accordance with the UK Copyright,
Designs, and Patents Act 1988.

All rights reserved. No part of this publication may be reproduced,
stored in a retrieval system, or transmitted, in any form or by any
means, electronic, mechanical, photocopying, recording or otherwise,
except as permitted by the UK Copyright, Designs, and Patents Act
1988, without the prior permission of the publisher.

First published 2008 by Blackwell Publishing Ltd

1   2008

Library of Congress Cataloging-in-Publication Data

Errington, James Joseph, 1951–
Linguistics in a colonial world : a story of language, meaning, and
power / Joseph Errington.
p.   cm.
Includes bibliographical references and index.
ISBN 978-1-4051-0569-9 (hardback : alk. paper) –
ISBN 978-1-4051-0570-5 (pbk. : alk.paper)
1. Linguistics–History. 2. Colonies. I. Title.

P71.E77 2007
410.9–dc22
2007014517

A catalogue record for this title is available from the British Library.

Set in 10.5 on 13 pt Palatino
by SNP Best-set Typesetter Ltd., Hong Kong

The publisher's policy is to use permanent paper from mills that
operate a sustainable forestry policy, and which has been
manufactured from pulp processed using acid-free and elementary
chlorine-free practices. Furthermore, the publisher ensures that the text
paper and cover board used have met acceptable environmental
accreditation standards.

For further information on
Blackwell Publishing, visit our website:
www.blackwellpublishing.com

Contents

List of Figures and Table

Preface

This is a book about European engagements with linguistic diversity in colonial projects around the world. It focuses on the ways colonial agents made alien ways of speaking into objects of knowledge, so that their speakers could be made subjects of colonial power. In this way it presents a language-centered survey of the colonial world from the 16th to the 20th century, showing how the work of linguistics changed in and with the projects of power it served.

At the same time, it is a story about the West's confrontation with linguistic diversity as a founding conundrum of the human condition, recasting the old question of what was once called the "confusion of tongues" (in Latin, *confusio linguarum*): the legacy of the fall of the Tower of Babel, told of in the book of Genesis, which was God's curse on the nations of humankind for their sin of pride.

Two thousand years ago, at the dawn of the Common Era, a philosopher living in Alexandria – an outpost of the Roman empire – gave the story of Babel an allegorical reading. This was Philo Judaeus, a Jewish student of Plato, who regarded his people's sacred texts as a kind of narrative shadow of God's Truth which he aimed to read on the wall of his worldly cave. Philo pointed out first how dubious was the story's literal meaning: it tells of linguistic diversity as a curse aimed at preventing humans from colluding again as they did at Babel, but even though "[m]en have been separated into different nations, and have no longer used one language, nevertheless, land and sea have been repeatedly filled with unspeakable evils. For it was not the languages which were the causes of men's uniting for evil objects, but the emulation and rivalry of their souls in wrong-doing" (1854:3). Philo went on to argue that God did not really create a confusion of tongues, but a division among them, making "one thing into many parts, as is the case when one distinguishes a genus into its subordinate species" (1854:41). These arguments capture two of this book's broadest themes.

Knowingly or not, willingly or not, colonial linguists carried out projects of physical and symbolic violence, some of them counting clearly as what Philo called "unspeakable evils." But they were also, knowingly or not, reducing to writing some of the evidence of a unity underlying linguistic and human diversity, charting properties shared among these "subordinate species," as Philo calls them, of the larger "genus" of language.

Always and everywhere, the work of linguistics in a colonial world was grounded in this enabling and conflicted condition, and the contradiction it presented for the work of power and knowledge. In a series of sketches I trace here linguists' ways of trying to disentangle languages from the communities and lives in which they figured, reading for the ways their dealings with language were enabled and shaped by their ideas about the human condition. By situating their projects of knowledge in larger projects of power, I try to show how the work of fixing languages in writing helped fix speakers in colonial yet "natural" hierarchies.

Acknowledgments

I am a linguist and anthropologist whose work straddles the study of language as a universal human attribute, and as part of the fabric of lives people create with each other. To move beyond my own special concerns with language use and change in Java, I have charted a course into unfamiliar intellectual, historical, and geographical territory. If I have managed to avoid writing like a rank dilettante, it is only because of the generosity of colleagues.

Some who have influenced me most are the least cited here: Chuck Briggs and Dick Bauman, Sue Gal and Judy Irvine, Jane Hill, Paul Kroskrity, Michael Silverstein, and Bambi Schieffelin. Kit Woolard has an inconstant correspondent's gratitude for her acuity and patience, and Hal Conklin my thanks not just for his invaluable example as a colleague, but for help with *baybayin*, the Philippine orthography I discuss in chapter 2. For the discussion of Nahuatl language and history there I am grateful to James Lockhart, more of whose expertise should probably have found its way into that same chapter.

My sketch of the political and cultural background of early linguistics in chapters 3 and 4 owes much to Michael Holquist, through both conversation and his work in progress on the beginnings of the Prussian system of education; Katya Benes generously discussed early German philology with me; Sara Pugach kindly allowed me to read what was at the time some of her unpublished work on Karl Meinhof. Discussion of Tamil in chapter 4 owes much to the advice and references at just the right time from my colleague Barney Bate, for which I am grateful.

Thanks also to David Dwyer for his help in disentangling some of the complexities of Shona in chapter 5, and Henk Maier for his help in different times and places to appreciate more fully the implications of his work on the history of Malay. I am grateful to Nina Garrett for improving an awkward Dutch translation, and to Shafqat Hussein for his dusty travails in the Mudd. Conversations with Doug Whalen and David Harrison helped me to frame difficult issues of language endangerment discussed in chapter 7. Finally, I am grateful to three anonymous readers for the care and spirit of generosity I found in their suggestions and criticisms. I hope my response gives adequate evidence of my appreciation for their help.

Finally, loving thanks for support in all times and places to my mother, Frances Clare Errington. This book is for her.

Joseph Errington

Chapter 1

The Linguistic
in the Colonial

The colonial era ended two generations ago, but colonialism has not really gone away. Its afterlife has been all too clear in global north–south inequalities; in bloody politics from Timor to Iraq to Rwanda; in critical identity politics where former colonial powers now are homes to former colonial subjects and their children. Many conspicuous signs of the colonial past in the globalizing present make it easy to wonder whether some genuinely new era is here or in the offing, or whether there has ever been a definitive rupture to separate us from the colonial epoch.

Some scholars have colonialism on their minds because they recognize that it might be in our minds, in the guise of durable categories and ideas which emerged then but still serve now as common sense for thinking about human diversity and inequality. These concerns have led many into closer, more critical engagements with textual remains of the colonial past, which they read with one eye on the present. History, biography, literature, and other kinds of writing take on new importance from this point of view, as do maps, censuses, photographs, monuments, and a wide range of other materials. All of these can be thought of as parts of a colonial archive: legacies of very different times and places which differ hugely in their form and content, are scattered over much of the world, but which all count as traces of the broad projects of power which accelerated and globalized between the 16th and 20th centuries.

The colonial archive was once primarily the territory of historians, but since 1970 or so they have been joined by other readers – in literature and intellectual history, anthropology and political science, comparative religion and psychoanalysis – who bring their own concerns and interests. Their agendas differ, as do the questions they pose and the parts of the archive which interest them, but some broad similarities can be seen between their strategies of critical reading. Beyond the archive's overt informational content and purposes, they read for broader understandings of the times and places in which those texts were produced so as to be useful and meaningful. Developing an imaginative sense of these texts, and reading them back into their contexts of origin, helps to make them windows on circumstances in which they could be useful, marginal, or dangerous; routine or innovative; and so on.

Reading for signs of authors' times – against the grain of texts, for what they say that their authors did not always intend – requires critical strategies for recognizing their partial vision, conflicted stances, changing perspectives, and mixed motives. When gaps or "silences" in the textual record are found – excluded facts, oversimple categories, elided stories, and so on – they can in turn be read diagnostically, as symptomatic of tensions which animated broader colonial projects, blurring lines between knowledge and interest, purpose and effect, between ideology and reality. In these ways power's shaping effects on the work of writing can be read back into what Louise Pratt calls "zones of colonial contact," and defines as "space[s] of colonial encounter . . . [as] peoples geographically and historically separated come into contact with each other and establish ongoing relations, usually involving conditions of coercion, radical inequality, and intractable conflict" (Pratt 1992:6)[1].

As a practical matter of fact, zones of contact were defined by lines of human difference bound up with language difference. Wherever colonial agents stopped short (as some did not) of brutal violence, they were obliged to find ways of bridging those linguistic gaps with acts of verbal communication, however rudimentary or inadequate. Talk was one of the lowest common denominators for colonial dealings when some humans made others targets of their efforts to persuade or awe, threaten or coerce, and who in turn resisted or cooperated, retreated or collaborated. Without "languages of colonial command" even simple ideas, orders, questions, threats, and arguments could not be communicated across these lines of colonial difference, which is why colonialists always and everywhere needed what Bernard Cohn (1996b) calls "command of colonial languages."

Given language difference as a fact of life in zones of colonial contact, in all times and places, it is not surprising that colonialists produced texts about languages over four centuries, around the world, or that those texts now represent a significant part of the colonial archive. It is likewise intuitively obvious that these sorts of texts – grammars, dictionaries, world lists, and so on – stand out because of their distinctive modes of organization and content. They count very obviously as reports on work which made languages objects of knowledge, so that their speakers could be made subjects of power.

But these texts are a trial to read because they also appear so opaque with respect to worlds of talk which they present in partial, written guises. They offer few clear points of purchase for critical readings against the empirical grain, back into the zones of colonial contact from which they emerged and which they so partially represent. The work of describing languages may require close engagement with complex intimacies of talk, but it results in texts which stand further from life's hard edges than many more institutional or official parts of the colonial archive: censuses or land surveys, photographs or revenue reports, even broad descriptions of "customs" or "ways of life."

This is a conundrum which rests on another. These dictionaries, grammars, and related texts present enormous amounts of descriptive information about enormously different languages, yet a quick perusal shows that they also resemble each other in obvious ways. Resemblances between these texts can be traced to the fact that each describes an object which falls under a single, common category. As a practical matter, linguists worked in zones of colonial contact on the premise that the languages they were describing could be compared with and presented in the image of others more familiar to them.

This conundrum of sameness-and-difference is important for framing larger meanings of the work of linguistics as a special kind of colonial encounter, and for reading very small bits of this part of the archive with an eye to its ideological, intellectual, and practical importance for prosecuting and legitimizing colonial projects.

Remembering that dry, minute descriptions emerged from situated dealings with conditions of human difference/sameness helps one to read them as part of the work of fixing colonial subjects in and with categories of colonial otherness. It allows this work to be considered as a means for adapting and exploiting familiar categories in ways which enabled power and legitimized authority in unfamiliar tongues.

Colonial Distance and Linguistic Difference

As projects of power, the work of linguistics I call "colonial" here served the "direct territorial appropriation of another geopolitical entity, and exploitation of its resources and labor, and systematic interference in the capacity of the appropriated culture . . . to organize its dispensations of power" (McClintock 1992:1). Most (not all) of this was work done by Europeans at considerable distances from the places where it was planned and authorized.[2] One influential approach to colonialism as a world historical phenomenon, then, is to read complex, scattered events four centuries into patterns of more and stronger flows of people and goods, capital, and technology around the globe. Up to the end of World War II, these political and economic dynamics gave rise to increasingly integrated geopolitical relations between European (and later American) centers of imperial power and scattered peripheries where that power was wielded.

From this angle, linguists can be regarded as a small, rather special group of colonial agents who adapted European letters to alien ways of talking and, by that means, devised necessary conduits for communication across lines of colonial power. However different the methods they used or objects they described, they transformed familiar alphabets into visual images of strange speech: their writing systems, or *orthographies*, were the common beginning point for the work of writing grammars, dictionaries, instructional texts, and so on.

But linguists who worked as technicians, transposing "our" alphabets onto blooming, buzzing confusions of talk, also served broader ideological projects. Always and everywhere, their written images of alien languages demonstrated underlying comparability:

once "their" talk was writable, like ours, resemblances were established between them and "us." This concrete commonality is obvious but also diffuse because it played out at shifting, slippery intersections between transient events of *talk*, what people *do*, and descriptions of *languages* which they share and which mark who they *are*, with and to each other.

This means that the intellectual work of writing speech was never entirely distinct from the "ideological" work of devising images of people in zones of colonial contact.[3] It means also that language difference figured in the creation of human hierarchies, such that colonial subjects could be recognized as human, yet deficiently so. Language difference in this way embodied some of the most basic "tensions of empire" which developed as colonialists had to "mark and police boundaries, design systems of punishment and discipline, [but also] to instill awe as well as a sense of belonging in diverse populations" (Cooper 2005:30). Written images of languages could embody these tensions, both constructing and giving a semblance of "naturalness" to other categories of colonial difference.

One way to read this work, then, is with an eye to the different hierarchies – religious, philosophical, evolutionary, and so on – which played into the ways it was done in different contexts, for different purposes. This leads also to readings of this work not just as it was written in zones of colonial contact abroad, but as it was read in Europe's metropolitan centers, circulating and figuring in larger ideological and intellectual challenges which colonial expansion continually posed. These were challenges not just to European understandings of linguistic and human diversity far away in the colonies, but at home, among colonizing nations.

I develop two different stances to this work of linguists. One is to regard them as technicians who deployed alphabetic symbols to "stand for" sounds of speech in unfamiliar tongues, and then devised descriptions of the meaningful elements those sounds comprised. The other is to read those texts as the work not of technicians of literacy but members of literate groups whose work was enabled and shaped by their social biographies, their broader investments in larger projects, their membership in certain groups, their broader beliefs, values, and purposes. From this second point of view, linguistic descriptions appear as points of convergence between stubborn empirical particulars and diffuse, powerful habits of thought and action. To read these works without forgetting that their authors were never *just* linguists can make them speak to the rootedness of that work in broader *practices of literacy*, and through those practices in the legitimizing textual traditions of faith and civilization.

Reducing Speech to Writing

A linguist can still read with profit old grammars, dictionaries, and similar texts because, as I noted above, they stand together with each other in the colonial archive, and share an expository logic which is evident in descriptive details about languages like those I discuss here, spoken in 17th century Mexico and the Philippines, 18th century India, 19th century Europe, 20th century Africa and Asia. The organizational coherence of these texts can be understood in two different ways.

From the empirical, "common sense" point of view, texts resemble each other as do the things they describe. This can be framed in terms of the guiding principle of modern linguistics: that specific languages exemplify a panhuman language faculty, a genetic endowment which grounds distinctively human ways of producing and understanding verbal communicative behavior. From the more critical point of view which allows for reading these texts "against the grain," resemblances between them are due to the techniques and strategies used to re-present languages in them. Texts are similar to each other, by this argument, because each presents such a partial image of diverse realities of talk. These opposed points of view, "empirical" and "critical," help here to develop a productive tension between readings of linguistic descriptions, one which it is worthwhile to articulate more fully through this section's usefully ambiguous title: "Reducing speech to writing."

Fifty years ago, linguists I discuss in chapter 7 often used this phrase to describe their work, and in so doing affirmed that it captured the empirical reality of properties of language *systems*. These are understood to be the abstract, internally organized, conventional linkages which, when embodied in talk, join sound with meaning. From this point of view, the colonial forebears of modern linguists were able to capture parts of a reality whose underlying nature they did not really understand when they thought of it as the legacy of the curse of Babel, an outgrowth of a natural environment, an organism which was fated to live and die in historical time, and so on. Beyond all these conceptions of language, which I discuss here, their work has value because it keyed to the ontological status of language systems, which have the thingy-ness of all natural phenomena.

From this empirical point of view, then, visual symbols map not just onto sounds of speech as tongues produce and ears hear them; they represent components of "underlying" language systems which talk embodies in order to be meaningful. In this sense linguists "reduce" speech to writing by capturing its underlying essentials, as they recur wherever and whenever talk happens. The better the alignment a linguist creates between sound and meaning, accurately representing them together within a language system, the more closely he or she cuts at the joints of that language's nature, whether it is spoken in 16th century Mexico or 21st century Indonesia.

A broadly contrary, critical view can also be summarized with the other sense which can be given to the phrase "reducing speech to writing." More philosophical arguments can be made that what linguists actually do is reduce the reality of language, which is talk, to their own timeless, airless realm of visual images. This is reduction as the work of substituting simplified part for complex whole, work which can seem straightforward and "natural" for linguists, and other literate people, only thanks to shared habits of thought and practice in writing. These habits lead them (and others) to ignore the constant gap which they create between verbal realities and visual representations.

Ludwig Wittgenstein mounted one such argument by observing that it is in the nature of humans (including linguists) to think that they are "tracing the outline of [a] thing's nature [here, a language] over and over again," when they are in fact "merely tracing around the [literate] frame through which [they] look at it" (Wittgenstein 1953:48). He arrived at this conclusion after he abandoned a philosophical project which had been founded on ideas about language broadly similar to those outlined above, whose designers had intended to capture universal properties of all languages with "an exact calculus," devised and used in the manner of "the sciences and in mathematics" (1953:25). Critical reflection led Wittgenstein to reject this project along with one of its basic premises: that the meaning of talk has the kind of stability which allows it be abstracted away and captured in written re-presentations.

With a series of simple thought experiments, Wittgenstein tried to demonstrate, not explain, that philosophers (and linguists) constantly make recourse to what they know, without having been taught, to describe language as separate from language use. Abstracting out writable elements that are the *same* in different acts of speech, they ignore the larger conditions in which those acts occur: conditions which are *shared* by those who are present for acts of speech. Wittgenstein foregrounded the meaningfulness of talk which depends on what people know, and know others know, about the times and places where it happens. These extend to broadly practical senses they can share but not necessarily describe about "what is going on" during, but also before and after, any given act of talk. Wittgenstein describes these senses of sharedness as "language games" which shape talk's situated meanings, and the conditions in which humans are with each other as speaking animals.

In his study and garden, Wittgenstein ruminated on these issues far from the messy details of exotic languages, or cruel realities of colonial encounter. But he drew attention to the kinds of habits of thought and practice which enabled and shaped the work of the colonial linguists I describe here. A broadly similar critique developed by Jacques Derrida (1976) can be mentioned here because it was directed more specifically at foundational work in the modern science of linguistics, which I discuss in chapter 7. Derrida applied his deconstructive technique to Saussure's writings by turning one of its founding premises on its head: the principle that the letter is secondary to the reality of speech and voice, which it represents. Linguists take this as an enabling principle: their orthographies count as surrogates used to create models of the primary reality of talk. But, Derrida argues, they proceed on the opposite premise because, when they assert that writing is secondary to speech, they also act as if there can be nothing in writing which is not already in what it describes. This means that if orthographies can represent stable patterns of sound and meaning, then those patterns must be part of the reality to which they are secondary. In fact, Derrida argues, this is the way linguists "read back" into speech a stability of meaning which actually exists only in their descriptions, the "secondary" realm of the letter.[4]

To make Derrida echo Wittgenstein in this oversimple way helps to frame very broadly some of the specific issues I deal with here as they emerged in the work of colonial linguistics. Unlike those philosophers, I share other linguists' senses of engagement with realities which one can work, more or less successfully, to "get right" in a description. But, as a critical reader of that work, I recognize not just that it is by its nature highly partial, but also the result of more than the observation of data and application of reason. It represents instead the product of language games which linguists (and other interested parties) adapted and devised in the face of specific challenges, and in response to practical needs.

So to read the work of colonial linguistics empirically and critically, I seek out strategies linguists used to arrive at part-for-whole substitutions of written images for linguistic realities, and the highly interested, power-laden positions from which they did this work. For this I need a narrower angle of vision than Wittgenstein's or Derrida's, and more situated ways of tracing the work of devising linguistic images in complex situations. To see how linguists extracted legible linguistic sameness from exotic human sharedness, I need to consider the ways they did not just devise orthographies, but adapted *practices of literacy*.

Practices of Literacy

The most basic way to read linguistic treatises not as records of facts, but as products of interests and imaginations, is to foreground the strategies of selection – always needed, and never disinterested – which went into the production of simple images of linguistic diversity. Two different strategies of selection were needed to create two kinds of part-for-whole substitutions, each oriented to a different sphere of the social meanings which talk has. One emerges from the ways differences in speech mark differences in speakers' identities, biographies, and community membership; the other emerges from the ways speaking fits into and molds people's senses of identity in face-to-face dealings with each other.

Issues of linguistic identity and background can be easily and oversimply thought of as matters of "dialect" and "accent," but these are terms which disguise and straddle complex, overlapping social categories: region, race, ethnicity, religion, class, gender, age, and so on. Such linguistic differences, always facts of social life, were encountered by colonialists as challenges which they dealt with by selecting some ways of speaking as their objects of description, while ignoring others. The ways they chose to make one way of speaking stand for many was always shaped by broader factors and purposes, allowing questions to be posed about what guided their strategies of selection, whether they knew it or not. What assumptions, interests, beliefs, and purposes shaped the ways they devised models *of* speech which could then be used as models *for* speech?

A second dimension of complexity emerges in the ways people's sense of themselves and others shifts with the talk which is part of their condition of being together. "Style" is the convenient, overeasy label for the molding of people's intersubjective orientations as "I" and "you" for each other in talk, perhaps in the presence of others. In these spaces of sharedness Wittgenstein's "language games" are in play, and speech can modulate them in ways more complex and subtle than can be conveyed with labels like "formal" and "informal," "respectful" or "familiar," "literate" or "colloquial."

Both of these kinds of linguistic complexity can be regarded as secondary from a literacy-centered view of language, each a kind of "add on" to the real business of talk: communicating information, expressing intent, and so on. But that complexity is important here because the step from facts of language difference to ideas about human deficiency is very short, and so questions of "dialect" and "style" played simultaneously into power-laden zones of colonial contact, and the politics of interaction. Strategies of selection, as linguists devised and used them, played indirectly but sometimes crucially into constructions of colonial power and authority.

These were engagements, then, which required resources that were more than technical and intellectual; they were shaped by broader senses of who people/speakers are to each other which linguists (among others) brought to their work. These can be called, as by the political philosopher Charles Taylor, their *social imaginaries*: the "normal expectations that we have of one another, the kind of common understanding which enables us to carry out the collective practices that make up our social life . . . [our] sense of how things usually go . . . interwoven with an idea of how they ought to go, of what missteps would invalidate the practice" (Taylor 2002:106, see also 2004). Though Taylor is concerned primarily with political culture and social change in modern Europe, his broad notion of "social imaginary" helps here to deal with the tacit, practical, background understandings which enabled linguists' work at the same time as they were disconfirmed or thrown into doubt by confrontations with radically different ways of being human in zones of colonial contact.

Taken-for-granted "expectations," "understandings," and "collective practices" are of interest here because linguists, as literate members of societies "back home," extended them in confrontations with alien languages. To become literate persons they were drawn into certain institutions, were members of particular groups, and had investments in the same textual traditions, religious and secular, which legitimized colonial projects. They shared habits of thought and belief with others who found what they wrote meaningful and useful for their own purposes, because it partook of a broader, shared sense of how writing and language use "usually" and "should" go.

To trace these social imaginaries as enabling and shaping the work of linguistics in zones of colonial contact, it is useful to foreground linguists' *practices of literacy*. "Practice" has become a term of art used by social scientists to emphasize the hidden power of habitual dispositions as shapers of much that is "automatic" and prereflective in human conduct, and so of textures of social life which lie beyond the purview of conscious, "rational" thinking.[5] So, too, for linguists to impose their habits of reading and writing on alien talk they also had to transpose and transform their literacy-related values, habits, and beliefs.

Practices of literacy have become a major research concern in a number of fields in recent years, but in this book I make use of two broadly opposed views of its nature. One, broadly aligned to the empirical stance to language outlined above, is the "common sense" view that literacy is a neutral means for representing characteristics of languages which are independent of it. Literacy then has the same essential logic and character in all times and places as a "technology of the intellect." I explore this idea further in chapters 2 and 3 as one of the grounds for the work of colonial linguists. The other view, more critical or "ideological," as Brian Street (1984) puts it, frames literacy's "particular manifestations" as they are embedded in "activities, events, and ideological constructs" (Besnier 1995:5). This view of literacy broadly parallels the view of language I sketched above as always bound up with contexts, and as something to be understood through particular acts and products, always "interact[ing] with ideologies and institutions to shape and define the possibilities and life paths of individuals" (Baynham 1995:71).[6]

Both of these views can help to trace linguists' understandings of their work, and the practical and ideological needs they addressed within larger colonial projects. Both help consider how linguists' work had meanings and uses which outstripped their own purposes and understandings, taking on lives of their own when, as texts, they circulated among different readers in different societies, and served different projects.

Linguistics between Faith and Civilization

The practices of literacy of interest here were bound up with textual traditions which lent legitimacy to colonialism more generally: of faith colonialists could seek to spread among pagans, and of civilization they sought to bestow on primitives. From the 16th through the 20th century, the deep textual roots of traditions of salvation and enlightenment were constantly invoked to justify brutal regimes, invasive projects, and pervasive hierarchies. So they figure in my historical sketch insofar as they were ways of making the work of linguists useful and authoritative. Whether they believed they were redressing God's curse on Babel, achieving minor versions of the miracle of Pentecost, or spreading the fruits of reason, linguists could refer their dealings with exotic particulars to transcendent values grounded in traditions and practices of literacy.

Such ideals can only be durable if they are continually reinvented and adapted across eras and colonial projects, and so also in the work of different colonial linguists. Under the rubric of faith, then, I trace the shifting purposes and values of linguistic descriptive work as it was done by Catholic missionaries in the 17th century (discussed in chapter 2), Protestants in the 19th century (described in chapter 5), as well as their postcolonial counterparts (chapter 7). These linked sketches of practices of literacy also help tie the work of these linguists at the peripheries of power to the broadest contours of change in Europe, where shifts in these same practices of literacy were bound up with the character of colonial projects from before the Reformation, through the industrial age, up to and past the era of high imperialism.

Faith drew so many to the work of conversion that missionaries count as the group which has produced the single largest body of knowledge about linguistic diversity around the world. I discuss two of the earliest of these projects in chapter 2, with a few of the dry details which make this kind of writing such a trial to read. But by drawing on work by friar linguists in two colonial settings – speakers of Nahuatl in Mexico, and Tagalog in the Philippines – I try to gauge the capabilities of these men of letters to shake their ears and minds loose from habits of thought to engage the linguistic face of colonial otherness.

But to the extent any such work is approached with habits of reading as much "to hand" and "natural" for us as those of the linguists who wrote them, it is difficult to develop a sense of how radically different the world of those friars was four centuries ago. Because it is important to try to bracket those habits of thought, a good beginning point for this story is the era when the practices of literacy which were their inheritance first developed. That is why my story begins with events dating from well before the dawn of the colonial era, when Charlemagne ruled in God's name in premodern western Europe.

During the 18th and 19th centuries, many linguists were Protestant missionaries with fundamentally different projects of the spirit that were enabled by different beliefs, technologies, and forms of colonial power. Their linguistic work needs to be described not just in the context of changing forms of faith, but of technology and especially the first European science of language.

Philology's Linguistic Images

Linguists in general, and missionaries in particular, partly described and partly created print-literate forms of colonial languages thanks to the ideological and intellectual support offered by comparative philology, a field which developed over the course of the 19th century. That field was shaped by ideas and values which later became ideologically and intellectually important for the work of colonial linguists, which is why I discuss philology's development in chapters 3 and 4 as an important dimension of the rise of linguistics, not just at colonial peripheries, but in the colonial world.

Thinking of colonialism as the global integrative dynamic mentioned above makes it easy to think that it emanated unidirectionally, and more and more forcefully, from metropolitan centers to scattered peripheries. This is an image which can confirm the view of civilizational progress held by those who prosecuted and most benefited from colonial projects. But at least since Edward Said's critical reading of European intellectual history, *Orientalism* (1994), it has become apparent that this image is itself part and parcel of that ideology. Said was among the first to search the colonial archive for evidence of power's shaping effects on knowledge and intellectual discourse. Reading in the manner of Michel Foucault, but less eurocentrically,[7] Said argued that the great archive of European knowledge about the Orient counted as an indirect but ideologically crucial response to the cultural and existential anxieties which arose from intimate engagements with colonial otherness. Reading like Franz Fanon, but from "above," not "below," Said worked to demonstrate that what seemed a stable, "objective" body of European knowledge of the Orient was in fact the history of engagements with the anxieties of human diversity, ". . . a continuous interpretation and reinterpretation of their differences from 'us'" (Said 1994:331–332).

The linguistic face of human diversity had always figured in debates about questions of human origins, and so knowledge of languages written by linguists abroad could travel back to Europe and into debates which joined questions of human origins and diversity with ideologies of European superiority. The role of linguistics in this intellectual and ideological project is so important that I devote chapter 3 of this book to two figures whose writings in the late 18th century shaped the broader meanings and uses of language difference in the 19th century. I discuss there early strategies devised for what Said describes as excavating and appropriating the "deep" history of colonized peoples, focusing on the great linguist and colonial officer of India, Sir William "Oriental" Jones. Though Said knew Jones' work, he passed over this foundational example of how a language-centered picture could be developed of linguistic, textual, and civilizational "decay" among a literate but inferior people. So, too, Said largely passed over philology's development as a field which Jones inspired. This is interesting here because it poses a conundrum for Said's broader account of orientalism's colonial origins.

Chapter 4 discusses the ways that philology, which was to become a cornerstone in the edifice of Orientalist knowledge, developed in Prussia at a time when it was the one major European power not yet invested in colonial projects abroad. Later in life, Said reproached himself for having passed in silence over the work of German-speaking intellectuals in *Orientalism*, noting that during most of the 19th century Prussia had no "protracted sustained *national* interest in the Orient" (Said 1994:19, emphasis added). But it is interesting that German-speaking intellectuals were just those Europeans who were developing dominant ideas about language, history, and identity which served their nation-building project at home, rather than a project of colonial power abroad.

It is worth emphasizing, then, that a European science of language helped to legislate national difference in Europe as well as human inequality in an imperial world. By drawing on recent, intellectual historical work which partakes of Said's own critical humanistic spirit, I use this book's middle chapters to frame the development of the science of language which, once established as a very European academic discipline, could be a source of ideological and intellectual support for colonial linguists abroad.

Colonial Regimes of Language

It is important to show how philological images of the past shaped the work of colonial linguists in the 19th and early 20th centuries, which I sketch in chapters 5 and 6. These missionaries sought to describe languages in order to create literate colonial subjects, which meant that they transposed practices of literacy from European nations to "native" communities. To describe the work they did and their "fields of operation" abroad, I draw on *Imagined communities*, Benedict Anderson's (1991) influential account of print-based literacy, senses of community, and the grounding of both in senses of national language and territory. This helps to show how missionary linguists created written images of languages in and with images of their speakers, mapping both for colonial regimes of power. Philological techniques and ideas helped them to appropriate languages descriptively, before "giving them back" to speakers in print-literate form. I demonstrate this intimate mode of entry into local lives with sketches of a few such projects undertaken in sub-Saharan Africa, where missionary linguists created the unitary languages they needed as instruments of religious conversion. Comparing neighboring projects helps to show how different linguistic communities could arise from this work, once colonial linguists made languages into means for "conceptualizing, inscribing, and interacting [with speakers] on terms not of their own choosing" (Comaroff and Comaroff 1991:15).

Chapter 6 turns to two quite different projects of fully imperial linguistics, each beginning at the turn of the 20th century, and each responding to the political and economic demands of two imperial structures. In territories of the Congo ruled by Belgium, and the East Indies ruled by the Netherlands, imperial integration made linguistic diversity a growing impediment, such that linguists were delegated to partly describe and partly create non-European languages of European power: Swahili and Malay were languages of state in the sense that neither had many native speakers on either side of the imperial divide.

On one hand, these two projects of colonial linguists stand out as intellectual and technical accomplishments, and as the clearest evidence of European capacities to impose unity in the face of diversity. Swahili and Malay became effective instruments of power only thanks to the expertise of those who fixed them descriptively, and the capacity of colonial institutions to transmit those languages, along with broader literacy practices, among colonial subjects. Those projects now have legacies in postcolonial nation-states (the Congo, Kenya, Tanzania, and Indonesia) where Swahili and Malay (now known as Indonesian) are spoken as national languages.

On the other hand, as Johannes Fabian has shown, these intellectual and technocratic projects were shot through with tensions of empire which could not be resolved, but only disguised and displaced. By framing Fabian's insightful account of the history of Swahili in the Congo with an eye to the work of imperial linguistics in the Netherlands East Indies, I show how Malay also figured in indirect responses to the broader dilemmas of imperial identity, and so had unintended uses in and consequences for imperial power. Bringing the linguistics of Swahili and Malay together helps gauge the broader limits of the power which colonial linguists served. Though they could describe and impose languages of power, they could not control their uses: colonial subjects, once "given" those print-literate languages, pirated them for their own purposes and projects of resistance.

Making this book fit the broad historical contours of colonial history brings me, in chapter 7, to the questions posed above about colonialism's afterlife in a globalizing present. That is why I conclude by considering the integrative dynamic of what now counts as globalization, and conditions of linguistic diversity in marginal groups' ongoing engagement with the encroaching power of postcolonial nations. To read the "flattening" effects of globalization on language diversity, I draw on earlier chapters to foreground postcolonial linguists' continuing involvement with broader questions of power and identity, obliging those who do that work to consider new versions of older questions about its meanings and uses.

Precolonial Prelude: Alcuin's Literacy

I introduced the paired notions of "practices of literacy" and "social imaginaries" above as a way of beginning to read linguistic texts within the lives, social backgrounds, and interests of those who wrote and read them. The idea of "practice" helps in this way to foreground the embeddedness of what people do in communities, political dynamics, and institutional contexts, which is why it is less useful to define it in abstract terms than to illustrate its application in particular situations. Recognizing and drawing out the importance of practices of literacy from their multiple embeddings is best done, in turn, by identifying conditions in which they conflict, differ, and change. During one such period, transformations of religious and secular authority also gave rise to practices of literacy that served the linguists I describe in chapter 2 six hundred years later. Their work of conversion in the 16th century in this way was rooted in textual traditions and practices of literacy of an older project of faith and power.

Histories of colonialism and linguistics often begin with the publication in 1492 of Anton de Nebrija's grammar of Castillian (Spanish) for two reasons: it was the first printed grammar of a "living," spoken language, and its author reportedly commended it to Queen Isabel with the infamous observation that "[l]anguage was always the companion of empire.... language and empire began, increased, and flourished together" (Trend 1944:88). No clearer charter could be given for linguistics as a part of any colonial enterprise, especially given that Columbus embarked that same year on his first voyage of discovery at Queen Isabel's behest.

But this remark is also significant for the ways Nebrija drew on the past to speak of the future. His humanist contemporaries would have recognized echoes in his observation of an earlier famous linguistic description, written in and about Latin – still a language of power – in 1441 (Lorenzo Valla's *Elegantiae linguae Latinae* [1488]). Among the empires Nebrija may have had in mind with his remark was that of Charlemagne (742–841 CE), the illiterate emperor who transformed Christian practices of literacy, and through them the religion itself.

When Charlemagne was crowned in 800 CE, Latin's unity as a language centered more on its textual than its oral forms, because "literacy" at that time was more than the skill of reproducing speech sounds in accordance with written letters. To be literate then was rather to be able to convey with speech the meanings of words written in characters for people who did not necessarily understand them unless they were put "in their own terms."

A Latin text in standard international orthography could be read aloud to listeners (in church, in law court, in the marketplace or for

literary entertainment) in whatever form and with whatever modifi-
cations were needed to be comprehensible. (Smith 1999:73)

This practice of literacy, fundamentally different from Nebrija's
and our own, involved no clear line between the activities we call
"reading" and "translating": pronouncing a text on the one hand,
or recasting its meaning in some other vernacular speech on the
other. Before Charlemagne, "[s]pelling out of the letters that cor-
respond to the sounds of a long-dead language" was less important
than the "transformation of the lines into their own living speech"
(Illich and Sanders 1988:60). These older practices of literacy also
differed from ours in that they required no distinction to be drawn
between the Latin language on one hand, and what we call the
Romance languages (French, Spanish, Italian, Catalan, Rumanian)
on the other.

Charlemagne took steps as God's servant to purify religious
practice and textual traditions by doing away with these shifting,
plural voicings of the Word. He saw that a new way of reading was
needed so that texts, the doctrine they conveyed, and the religious
practices they supported were fixed and stable. The clergy were to
act as mediators between God and the faithful by transforming
silent letters into audible speech in the same ways, by the same
rules, thus guarding religious truth from the dangers of translation,
and distortion, in any vernacular, "rustic" manner (Illich and
Sanders 1988:61).

Alcuin the Scot, Charlemagne's servant in this matter, was a
scholar-priest from Northumbria, England, who came to this task
as an outsider; because he did not speak any of the Romance languages (*lingua Romana*) natively, he was free of habits of speech
which might skew his work to reduce Latin to uniformity.[8] (In this
regard his "outsider" position as a linguist anticipated that of many
of the linguists I discuss in this book.) The implications of his work
for the politics of religion were not lost on the Church, as became
clear at the Council of Tours. When Charlemagne urged the gathered bishops to accept his reforms some resisted, appealing to the
Pentecostal miracle; some likely foresaw that the ascendance of
letter over voice, and repetition over translation, would transform
the priesthood. As local practices of literacy and ritual became
delegitimized, priests became progressively distanced from their

audiences, as were texts and doctrine which became opaque to all but the literate few.

Alcuin the Scot is an important figure for this story about colonial linguistics in two ways. First, his work demonstrates the power of practices of literacy, which is thrown into relief by the ways they change in and with the meanings, uses, and authority of textual traditions. Second, with his work were promulgated the practices of literacy which were inherited and adapted by Valla, Nebrija, and other scholars in Spain, although these only became fully established and authoritative as late as 1200 CE and adapted for writing Castillian speech as late as 1252 (Smith 1999:74).

Perhaps Nebrija's pronouncement marked his recognition that power was best served by a "symbolically effective, uniform, imperial, dead language" (Illich and Sanders 1988:59). But it was his scholarly work on Latin which proved to be of greater practical importance for the friars who embarked for the New World. They engaged in projects of empire different from any he might have imagined, and with languages so different from their own that they posed challenges to faith, imagination, and intellect alike.

Notes to chapter 1

1   Pratt's phrase "zones of colonial contact" is especially appropriate in a book centered on language, since she took it over from "contact linguistics," the structure-centered study of the dynamics of language change.
2   That "colonial" power is commonly thought of as being exercised at a distance can be seen in common usage. Denmark's brief rule over islands in the West Indies is more appropriately called "colonial," for instance, than its centuries of dominance over nearby Iceland or Norway, if not more distant Greenland; Native Americans were victims of projects of violence and genocide as vicious as any in the world, but these are not usually called "colonial" except by scholars, who will usually qualify it with the label "internal colonialism," which is also applied to English domination of neighboring Ireland. In this respect the conquest of North America differed from American imperial rule in the Philippines and Puerto Rico after the Spanish–American war. Common use also suggests a eurocentric slant to "the colonial:" it seems a bit awkward as a label for the Moorish occupation of the Iberian

peninsula on the one hand, or Abyssinia's regime of power over the neighboring Oromo people, established at the same time and in broadly the same ways as those of Europe's powers in the rest of Africa in the 19th century.

3 Broad explorations of these issues from an ideological point of view can be found in Kroskrity (2000), especially Judith Irvine and Susan Gal's essay "Language ideology and linguistic differentiation."

4 For broadly similar arguments from vantage points still closer to linguistics, see Roy Harris's *The language makers* (1980) and *Language, Saussure, and Wittgenstein: how to play games with words* (1988). See also J. Joseph and T. Taylor's collection *Ideologies of language* (1990).

5 Two major figures who developed notions of "practice" are Pierre Bourdieu in works like *Outline of a theory of practice* (1977) and Michel de Certeau's *The practice of everyday life* (1984). Bourdieu argues in his work that linguists' portrayals of language, besides being inaccurate, have misled those who have used them as models for social conduct more generally. Other important work which brings notions of discursive practice to questions of language and power is Grillo 1989.

6 Of the literature on literacy, which has grown tremendously in the last 15 or 20 years, especially in history and education, I mention only Goody 1986 as a convenient setting out of the core ideas Street critiques as the "autonomous" model of literacy; Shirley Heath's (1983) early, influential ethnography of literacy in the contemporary United States, which helped to stimulate much ensuing research; and a recent synthetic review of that work by Collins and Blot (2003).

7 One could add to important work (for instance, Mitchell 1988, Stoler 2002) critiquing Foucault's (1970) eurocentric focus a commentary on his account of the idea of language, framed with an eye to the early work of colonial linguists I discuss in Chapter 2. That is a task beyond the scope of this book.

8 A much more detailed discussion of Alcuin's work can be found in Wright's (2003) sociophilological study of late Latin.

Chapter 2

Early Conversions, or, How Spanish Friars Made the Little Jump

It all goes back to conversion, Father, a most ticklish concept and a most loving form of destruction.
Louise Erdrich, *Last report on the miracles at Little No Horse* (2001)

In the 16th century, mendicant friars joined explorers and conquerors in the New World, and from there traveled across the Pacific to islands on the far side of the world. They did not understand theirs to be the work of enslaving, murdering, or displacing those they called in both places *indios*; it was rather to make them Christians. Because pagan ways of speaking were their chosen ways of entering pagan hearts, these friars required of themselves the difficult work, early and late, of converting living speech to alphabetic writing. I discuss here some of their engagements with alien languages, parts of the work of loving destruction which were foundational for European traditions of language study, and as such are still intelligible four centuries later.

The main goal of this chapter is to show how the work of fixing pagan speech in writing helped to locate pagan speakers in natural, spiritual, and political hierarchies. I do this by discussing two of these projects, carried out for similar purposes but in different zones of colonial contact. From these I need to draw just a few of the fine-grained details which friar linguists themselves took so seriously, exploring their efforts to bracket habits of speech, categories of knowledge, and so to use and understand alien languages as did their native speakers. Only in this way could they hope to capture strange talk's properties in their written texts, and then appropriate it for their own purposes in the "New France" of North America, "New Spain," Portugese South America, and many other places in the early colonial era.

This chapter deals secondly with this work's broader meanings and uses in early debates about the New World's human-like creatures, as it emerged from and figured into the Conquest's political and ideological grounding. Against the backdrop of early Spanish imperial ideology, these descriptions can be read as evidence of what friar linguists themselves recognized to be languages of humans who were to be saved for God, if not from other Europeans.

This chapter's third major purpose is to foreground the simplifying strategies which friar linguists developed to represent complex worlds of living speech with simple written images. In different zones of colonial contact, and engagements with speakers and speech, they encountered different challenges which we can read into work that served always and everywhere in lovingly destructive projects of conversion. In this way the reductive force of their linguistic descriptions can be understood as part of broader appropriations of pagan languages in order to supplant pagan ways of life.

It helps to frame these writings by friar linguists on Nahuatl and Tagalog opportunistically, as if they were produced in zones of colonial contact which mirrored each other. In Mexico, they recognized and used Nahuatl as the language of the dominant, civilized elite in a complex society, which nonetheless lacked anything they were willing to recognize as Nahuatl practices of literacy. In the Philippines, friar linguists saw Tagalog as the language of "primitive" people living in simple societies, but at the same time could not avoid recognizing that they also possessed indigenous practices of literacy.

To deal with this work in its own terms, with an eye to empirical particulars, I also opportunistically focus here on one speech sound which friar linguists were obliged to deal with in their descriptions of Nahuatl and Tagalog alike. This sound, called in Spanish the *saltillo*, or "little jump," was one they had to learn and write en route to appropriating the languages in which it figured. But their strategies for doing so differed as did the broader colonial projects in which their work was situated, and the broader projects of conversion they undertook.

Understanding the "Barbarian"

It might be as challenging for us to imagine the conundrums Europeans confronted after the discovery of the New World as it was for them to make sense of the distant, human-like creatures which were encountered there. Politically and religiously fraught questions about humanity, "theirs" and "ours," were constantly entangled with European projects of conquest, questions which from the beginning joined ideas about the nature of humans and the nature of language.

Early accounts of these early explorations have led two critical readers to suggest that at the outset of this encounter, Europeans were unable to categorize their experiences of peoples of the New World in stable, consistent ways. Tvetzvan Todorov, for instance, finds in Christopher Columbus's narrative of his first voyage a kind of split vision of an alien human condition: he could either "acknowledge [native speech] as a language but refuse to believe it [was] different" from his own, or he could "acknowledge its difference but . . . refuse to admit it [was] a language" (Todorov 1984:29).

Other records of early explorers led Stephen Greenblatt to a similar interpretation of an unstable binary perception of human-like creatures and the language-like sounds they produced. He sees the shaping effects of a will to power in shifting perceptions of the New World's peoples. Europeans had to "peel away and discard like rubbish" (Greenblatt 1990:32) what might otherwise be inconvenient linguistic evidence of the human nature, and so had recourse to one side or other of a rigid binary distinction. If speech-like sounds were judged to fall beyond the pale of language, then the creatures producing them fell beyond the pale of humanity, and issues of commonality need not enter into any calculation of advantage and obligation. But if those sounds were to be counted as instances of a human language, however opaque and meaningless, then their producers could be immediately assimilated not just to the category of human, but to European interests.

The cruelest example of this refusal of difference in the service of power was a document called the Requerimiento, which Spanish Conquistadores carried to the New World. The Requerimiento, drawn up (in Castilian) at the behest of King Ferdinand of Castille in 1513, was in the tradition of charters which the Vatican had begun to issue ten years earlier, requiring soldiers of Christ to destroy those who refused His love (Moors and Jews on the Iberian peninsula, later *los indios* in the New World). In this way the Requerimiento extended the tradition of the Crusades, and Castille's own recent reconquest of Granada, a battle for Christ closer to home which became a model for Cortez's expedition to Mexico in 1519, and Pizarro's to Peru, where he murdered king Atuahalpa in 1532.

The Requerimiento is worth discussing here because it was bound up with practices of literacy which seem bizarre enough now to require our own imaginative engagement with unfamiliar ideas about power, writing, and speech. The document was to be read aloud in the presence of *los indios* so as to inform them that, through that act of reading, they were bound either to submit to the king of Spain and the Christian church, or suffer consequences which the reader of the document went on to describe. What seems a strange mixture of duty and cynicism, at least for us, depends on a refusal of linguistic difference: the enabling presupposition was that (prototypically male) creatures who heard it but did not understand its import were therefore subhuman, and so could be subjugated forthwith:

> [w]e shall take you and your wives and your children, and shall make slaves of them, and as such shall sell and dispose of them as their Highnesses may command; and we shall take away your goods, and shall do you all the mischief and damage that we can, as to vassals who do not obey, and refuse to receive their lord, and resist and contradict him; and we protest that the deaths and losses which shall accrue from this are your fault, and not that of their Highnesses, or ours, nor of these cavaliers who come with us. And that we have said this to you and made this Requisition, we request the notary here present to give us his testimony in writing, and we ask the rest who are present that they should be witnesses of this Requisition. (Helps 1856(1):361)

These readings had meanings reaching far beyond anything Nebrija imagined when he commented on language and empire going together.

Denying *los indios* any presence as speaking and understanding beings made it easy to dispense with their physical presence for the reading of the Requerimiento as well:

> [i]t was read to trees and empty huts . . . Captains muttered its theological phrases into their beards on the edge of sleeping Indian settlements, or even a league away before starting the formal attack . . . Ship captains would sometimes have the document read from the deck as they approached an island. (Hanke 1949:33–34)

The Requerimiento can be taken as a kind of early prototype for linguistic asymmetries of colonial power: the nonintelligibility of speech provided sufficient grounds for subjugating them because it was evidence not of their difference, but their deficiency. Given the undeniable and self-evident meaningfulness of "our" speech, "their" inability to understand it revealed a more deeply flawed human condition. The grim absurdity of this logic was clear enough to some European witnesses; friar Bartolomeo de las Casas, who witnessed the reading of this document, found himself not knowing whether to laugh or cry.

In Spain the question of language was central for resolving the status of *los indios* so as to legitimize the Conquest. On his return there to decry to the king cruelties carried out in his name, de las Casas focused on this disputed category, protesting the willful refusal of linguistic difference and insisting that this condition of unintelligibility was at base mutual. Though natives of the New World might be called barbarians, he argued, that category is not absolute but relative:

> A man is apt to be called barbarous, in comparison with another, because he is strange in his manner of speech and mispronounces the language of the other . . . But from this point of view, there is no man or race which is not barbarous with respect to some other man or race. . . . Thus, just as we esteemed these peoples of these Indies barbarous, so they consider us, because of not understanding us. (De las Casas 1971:166)

"Barbarian," known to classically trained scholars of the time from Greek, was a word which was originally onomatopoeic, reproducing sounds which crude beings used (as the civilized Greeks saw it) in poor imitation of their own proper speech. Stammering, meaningless "barbar" sounds were then a sign of inferiority if not evaluated relativististically, as de las Casas did by invoking the words of no less a figure than St. Paul: "If I then know not the meaning of the voice, I shall be to him that speaketh a barbarian, and he that speaketh will be a barbarian unto me' (I Corinthians, 14.11). Behind the authority of the New Testament, in turn, lay that of the Old: the story of Babel and the confusion of tongues in Genesis, which explained linguistic difference as sinful humanity's common heritage. *Los indios*, like other descendants of those who fled the tower's fall, were inheritors of the common human curse. This was the original condition invoked by one friar linguist to describe his purpose: "to restore in part the common eloquence of which we were deprived by the arrogance and pride of that building" (quoted in Pagden 1982:181).

To refute de las Casas' relativistic understanding of "barbarian" speech and intelligibility, churchmen who had the king's ear drew on a different intellectual tradition, giving that word another meaning. They responded to Ferdinand's request for opinions on his right of conquest by arguing that fully human creatures are distinguished by more than a simple capacity for speech. The fully human condition is one of sociality which, in the classical tradition of city-dwelling Greeks, was understood to require a capacity for linguistic eloquence. Only through such eloquence could humans be induced to join each other in civilized conditions of hierarchy and comity. Here the churchmen invoked Cicero's famous argument that where eloquence is lacking, bonds of association can only be forged by brute force among creatures who fall short of a truly human condition (Pagden 1982:21).

Far away, in Mexico and Peru, the Conquistadores could be in no doubt that they were in fact destroying civilizations and subjugating civilized peoples; as the friar linguists I discuss later saw very clearly, in these societies people were distinguished by their capacities for eloquence. But reports about pagan civilizations and languages traveled poorly and had little purchase on those who chose to believe otherwise, as friar Bernadino de Minaya discovered on his return from Peru. He went

> begging, to Valladolid, where I visited the cardinal and informed him [about] the Indians' language . . . [and] their ability and the right they had to become Christians. He replied that I was much deceived, for he understood that the Indians were no more than parrots. (Hanke 1937:84)

It is easy to think that friars who recognized *los indios* as objects of Christian love, and witnessed their subjugation in the Conquest, brought a sense of urgency to their engagements with pagan languages. Their descriptions could count as massively detailed evidence of capacities for well wrought speech, and so for speakers' rights both to be converted to the Faith and protected by the king. In the dedication of his 1560 lexicon of Quechua, the language of the Incan empire, Friar Domingo de Santo Tomas addressed King Philip II to point out how "clearly and manifestly . . . false is the position of which many have sought to convince your Majesty, that the people of Peru are barbarians." On the contrary, Quechua was

> adorned with the regularity of declension and the other properties of the noun, and with the moods, tenses, and persons of the verb. In short, in many respects and ways of expression, it conforms to Latin and Spanish. The language is civilized and abundant, regular and ordered by the same rules and precepts as Latin, as is proved by this grammar. (Quoted in Macormack 1985:448)

A grammar itself counted as direct evidence of a civilized condition, and could be used to legitimize the work of conversion, giving pagans knowledge of Christ in words they understood. So argued a militant French Franciscan in a 1533 letter to Ferdinand's successor, Charles V, which chastised those who

> would not take the trouble of learning their language, and did not have the zeal to break that wall to enter their souls and search with candles for the wonders that God works in their hearts . . . [who should] now be silent and seal their mouths with bricks and mud." (Quoted in Tavárez 2000:22)

Between 1533 and 1620, the kings of Spain (Charles V and after him Philip II) ordered that *los indios* be given Castilian, the proper language of all their subjects. Their decrees were ignored by the friars because they were impractical, and did not serve their own, higher purpose. They knew *los indios* to be children of God who had not yet been corrupted by the world, and so could only be saved if they were insulated from the pride and greed of other Europeans. So they understood that

> for the Mexican to become a true Christian he had to break entirely with his past, except, and this is an important fact, in his language, because it was clearly understood that to become a true Christian he did not at all have to become a Spaniard, that it was perfectly allowable, and even recommended, that he remain a Mexican. (Ricard 1966:288)

With this observation, Ricard identifies that aspect of the friar's work of conversion which might fit least well with his own influential chronicle of these missionaries' "spiritual conquest" of Mexico.

Triangulating on Pagan Languages

The demands of faith and the realities of power both led

> [e]very missionary that came to the new world [to think] it his duty to write at least one grammar (*arte de la lengua*) during his life. By the middle of the sixteenth century there were enough grammars and prayer books written in various dialects to enable the clergymen to study them in the seminaries. (Campa 1931:549)

These missionaries saw *los indios* as objects of Christ's love, and heard their talk as writable language which they could turn to His purposes: they could not love what they did not understand, and so needed to find a fit between alien speech and their own categories of meaning. Only by appropriating speech with their own practices of literacy could they give a language back to its speakers as the medium of Christian discourse, and part of the gift of the Faith.

Missionaries could work in this way to redress what de las Casas himself acknowledged was *los indios'* "lack [of] a literary language which corresponds to their maternal idiomatic language, as is Latin to us, and thus [they] do not know how to express what they think" (de las Casas, quoted in Pagden 1982:130).

The Conquistadores modeled their exploits on the Crusades and the Reconquista of Spain; trade developed across the Atlantic thanks to expertise of older Mediterranean mercantile communities (see Laiou 1998). So too missionaries drew confidence and techniques from their own textual traditions. Though not practicioners of what we would call a "linguistic science," their work was rooted in the traditions of knowledge of what they called (in Latin) *scientia,* following Aquinas' observation that "[w]e all have to learn to interpret what we see, and this can only be achieved through the use of books" (Pagden 1982:130).

Nebrija influenced these first friar linguists less through his famous grammar of Castilian than through his earlier grammar of Latin, written in Latin, in 1481 (the *Introductiones Latinae*). His explanation of Latin's grammatical categories in that book became indispensable for friars' first attempts to generalize about the New World's vastly different languages. They

> understood that the traditional Latin grammatical framework needed to be modified to accommodate them, but they faced a dilemma. On the one hand, if they forced these languages into the Latin mould they knew that they would be distorting the facts; but on the other hand, if they abandoned that framework altogether they would run the risk of finding themselves in completely uncharted territory. (Perceval 1999:19)

But the grammatical knowledge they were applying was embedded in broader practices of literacy, and in traditions of meaning and belief which invested their grammars with values. Vincent Rafael's study of early descriptions of Tagalog, which I consider in more detail later in this chapter, helps to develop a sense of the hierarchy of literacies and languages which friars brought to their work in the New World as well.

Rafael suggests that Tagalog could become a descriptive object only as it came to be located in hierarchical relations to Latin as a descriptive model, and Castilian as a descriptive instrument. Unlike Perceval, who emphasizes Latin grammar's intellectual usefulness for these friar linguists, Rafael points to the broader meanings of Latin in textual embodiments of sacred truth (thanks to the practices of literacy established by Alcuin centuries before). Borrowing from Benedict Anderson's observations about social imaginaries in a world of limited literacy, Rafael suggests that Latin counted for these friars as a "Truth language," one which stands apart from mundane speech and life as a "privileged system[s] of [written] representation" (Anderson 1991:14). Latin partook, part-for-whole, of the sacred power of the messages it conveyed; it was not just a vehicle of meaning but a kind of emanation of the source of meaning, God's "superterrestrial order of power" (Anderson 1991:13).

Castilian, for its part, served as a language which could mediate, textually and ideologically, between text-based sacred Latin and oral pagan speech. Rafael suggests that in the work of description Castilian served to deploy a conceptual apparatus or metalanguage grounded in Latin. More than a (spoken) language of secular power, Castilian took on legitimacy from its proximity and similarity to the language of transcendent truth. Rafael reads this authorizing symbology of faith and power from work of friar linguists in the Philippines which I discuss later, but his insight is also suggestive for considering other zones of contact in which friar linguists dealt with pagans and their talk. However well they knew, as Perceval suggests, that they were deforming pagan languages to convert them to writing, they knew also that these loving deformations confirmed the fact of pagan languages' deficiencies in relation to "the intrinsic superiority of some languages – in this case Latin and Castilian – over others in the communication of God's Word" (Rafael 1993:29).

Nahuatl's Little Jump

Beyond broad questions of belief, power, and faith lay the descriptive particulars which consumed much time and required much attention for these first linguists. I consider here some of the first, formative parts of the work of description they undertook in the spirit of Alcuin: establishing regular relations of letters and voice so that fixed, inspectable written images could come to be models of and for speech. Of interest here is the intimate zone of contact where sounds of Nahuatl met friars' ears before they put pen to paper to map that language with their own alphabetic symbols.

Walter Mignolo's critical readings of some of their work lead him to conclude that this painstaking work was not just shaped but seriously deformed by habits of thought and practices of literacy, which friar linguists could not recognize or bracket. For them Latin was so fundamentally a "universal linguistic system," he argues, that they deployed its categories and letters normatively, not descriptively. Latin's superiority gave

> [t]he letter . . . an ontological dimension with a clear priority over the voice as well as any other writing systems. The classical tradition was inverted, and the letter . . . had become the voice in itself, while non-alphabetic writing systems were suppressed. (Mignolo 1995:46)

Mignolo reads in this work a kind of "violence of the letter," as Derrida puts it, which is of a piece with the Conquistadore's systematic destruction of Nahuatl practices of epigraphic literacy, a way of "writing without letters" which they neither understood nor tolerated.[1]

The more intimate symbolic violence done by these linguists can be seen, Mignolo argues, in the ways they applied Latin letters to Nahuatl. The "one letter, one sound" principle led them to perceive a "lack" of sounds in pagan languages. This reading of difference as deficiency is evident, Mignolo says, from the use of a "common and repeated expression in these early texts: *esta lengua carece de tales letras* (this language lacks such and such letters)" (1995:46). He illustrates this bias by quoting from a 1645 grammar of Nahuatl (*Arte de la lengua mexicana*) by the Jesuit missionary Horatio Carochi, who began by observing that "[t]his language is written with the letters of the Spanish alphabet, although it lacks seven letters, which are b, d, f, g, r, s, and j" (Carochi 2001[1645]:19). So profound and natural was the assumption of Latin's universality, Mignolo suggests, that in the very next sentence Carochi could contradict himself by urging care on his reader in learning to pronounce the Mexican language.

But a bit further on in the text Carochi seems less blinkered by orthographic habit, because he uses the word "letter" more flexibly and descriptively. He goes on to note that just as Mexican (i.e., Nahuatl) lacks "letters" found in Latin, so too it has a "letter" which Latin lacks:

> similar in pronunciation to z and c, but it is pronounced more strongly and corresponds to the Hebrew letter *tsade*; in this language it is written with t plus z, as in Nitzàtzi, I shout; Nimitznōtza, I call you; but it is a single letter, although written with two. (Carochi 2001[1645]:19)

In this passage Carochi alternates between two senses of the word "letter" which modern linguists can recognize. It is a rough and ready metalinguistic vocabulary which is less literal, as it were, than Mignolo suggests.

Carochi can describe "a single letter" as being "written with two" without contradicting himself because his first use of "letter" refers to a recurring pattern or type of sound which he has identified as common in Nahuatl speech, but which is dissimilar from any which are ordinarily (and conventionally) associated with Latin orthography. His second use of the word "letter" names a symbol which he stipulates will serve (conventionally) as the visual counterpart of that sound in his description. Because he alternates between these two senses – "speech sound" and "visual symbol" – he can stipulate that "a single letter" (a speech sound) is to be written "with two" (a combination of characters, what nowadays is called a digraph).

Carochi in fact triangulates on this sound by appealing to his readers' presumed knowledge of Hebrew, which happens to be useful in its own way thanks to spelling conventions which help him describe acoustic properties of a sound of Nahuatl. (Elsewhere in this work he draws on Hebrew grammar to describe Nahuatl affixes, as had his predecessor, del Rincón, in 1595.)

More interesting here, though, is another challenge posed by a "lack" in Latin orthography for writing a Nahuatl speech sound. Carochi called this sound the *saltillo*, or "little jump," and transcribed it with an apostrophe. (Nowadays it is called in English "glottal stop," and can be heard in English interjections written "uh-oh" or "uh-huh," using hyphens to mark the point at which

the air stream is briefly halted by closing the vocal cords, or glottis.[2])
To represent this sound in this text I use the character from the
International Phonetic Alphabet, whose origins I touch on in chapter
4: the glottal stop will be represented here with the symbol ʔ to
discuss friar linguists' dealings with the *saltillo* in Nahuatl, and also
in Tagalog.

Nahuatl's *saltillo* was of special concern for Carochi, not just as a
fact about speech, but an object of social value for its speakers:

> Whether to put a *saltillo* or a long accent rests on almost impercep-
> tible practices, so that not even those who are very expert in this
> language can manage to give the reason for the difference. Yet if it
> is not observed, it will be a barbarism and a very great impropriety.
> (Carochi 2001[1645]:267)

This remark is telling in several ways. First, it suggests a kind of
temporary inversion of linguistic and social hierarchies in a special
zone of colonial contact: here what is barbaric is not the speech of
los indios, but of Spaniards who fail to imitate them adequately.
Second, this comment on usage is grounded in broader concerns
with style of speech and speaker status, reflecting the broader social
hierarchies which I discuss below as having shaped missionaries'
work of spiritual conversion. But before discussing the Nahuatls
whom Carochi judged to be "very expert in this language," and
whose authority he borrows for his own description, it is useful to
turn first to the ways friar linguists dealt with Tagalog's *saltillo*,
which involved them not just with native speech, but native
writing.

Tagalog Sounds and Letters

Early explorers of Luzon and surrounding islands were struck by
the natives' use of

> certain characters [which] serve as letters with which they write
> whatever they wish. . . . The women commonly know how to write
> with them, and when they write, it is on some tablets made of the
> bamboos which they have in those islands, on the bark. In using such
> a tablet, which is four fingers wide, they do not write with ink, but

with some scribers with which they cut the surface and bark of the bamboo, and make the letters. (Quoted in Scott 1994:210)

That writing should exist at all in such remote locations was as remarkable as the fact that so many people, even women, mastered it.

These explorers could not know that they had reached a fringe of the vast area – stretching from Afghanistan to Java, Sri Lanka to Nepal, and beyond – where South Asian practices of literacy had been transmitted from the end of the first millennium up through the 13th or 14th century CE. In chapter 3 I discuss Britain's colonial encounters with Sanskrit, one of the oldest parts of this tradition, but here one of the newest of these scripts is important: one of nine known to have been in use on the islands of Visaya and Luzon, called in Tagalog *baybayin*.

Missionary linguists recognized that *baybayin* was a technique for imaging language in a manner similar to alphabetic writing. Both analogize sequences of sounds in time to linear successions of characters in space. This transposition can be read from the meaning of the word *baybayin*, derived from a root (*baybay*) which, in other words, serves to speak of ways one follows or traces a line (the bank of a river, the side of a street, a row or line of people, and the like).

Babayin, like related orthographies, differs from alphabetic writing in that each of its 18 "main" characters represents not a single sound but a syllable, that is, a combination of a consonant followed by a vowel. This important, basic difference is worth illustrating. The alphabet symbol *b*, for instance, is read as (represents) one sound except when pronounced as its own name ("the letter *b*"), a vowel is added (so, a sound sequence which is the same as that of the words *be* and *bee*). I need to avoid possible confusion here, and so adapt standard practice among linguists by representing this vowel in following discussion with the letter *i*. By this convention, the "ordinary" spelling of *be* and *bee* would be replaced with *bi*.

In *baybayin*, on the other hand, there is a symbol which corresponds to *b*, Ͻ, but which is always read with a following vowel. In its simple, unmodified form, this vowel is like that in the first syllable of the English word "father," which I transcribe here alphabetically

as *a*. So the Tagalog sound represented in *baybayin* by ꩜ corresponds to and could be written (transliterated) with letters of
the alphabet as *ba*. Other syllables which begin with *b*, but are followed by a different vowel, are written in *baybayin* by adding a
mark to the basic character ꩜. So the sound combination I transcribed as *bi* above would be written in *baybayin* by adding a mark
above it: ꩜.

With two symbols to mark vowels other than *a*, *baybayin*'s basic
characters can be used as an elegantly economical way to write 54
syllables, the majority of those found in Tagalog. But Tagalog has
a few relatively uncommon syllables which not only begin but end
(or close) with consonants.[3] *Baybayin* has no characters to represent
these speech sounds – *n*, *l*, and *k* – when they appear after a vowel
at the end of a syllable. This means that a Tagalog word which has
closed syllables like *bundul* (referring to an act of bumping or
ramming violently against something) is written with the same
baybayin characters as is the word *bunduk* (meaning "mountain," a
word borrowed into English as "boondocks"). The *baybayin* version
of these two words, transliterated directly into alphabetic writing,
is in both cases *budu*.

The friar linguists who first came to the island of Luzon
recognized this as point of deficiency in ways I discuss later, but
did not regard it as a reason to ignore *baybayin*. The earliest text in
Tagalog, the 1593 *Doctrina Christiana en lengua española y tagala*, sets
out basic texts and prayers translated into Tagalog, and written
with both Latin and *baybayin* characters. It can be read, then, as a
kind of primer to help friars learn Tagalog and *baybayin* together.
Missionaries also saw a way of "improving" *baybayin*. Thirty years
later a missionary who wrote the *Doctrina* in a neighboring language, Ilokano, introduced a device he saw as remedying this
deficiency:

> The reason for putting the text of the Doctrina in Tagalog type . . . has
> been to begin the correction of the said Tagalog script, which, as it
> is, is so defective and confused (because of not having any method
> until now for expressing final consonants – I mean, those without
> vowels) that the most learned reader has to stop and ponder over
> many words to decide on the pronunciation which the writer
> intended. (F. Lopez quoted in Scott 1994:215)

Lopez's device "improved" *baybayin* for his "most learned reader" – non-native speakers/readers, like himself – by aligning it more closely with Latin orthography. This mark – made in the image, fittingly enough, of the cross – was placed below a consonant symbol which was to be read without a following vowel. (In this way he unknowingly reinvented an orthographic convention common to related syllabaries used all across Asia, most famous among them the Sanskrit *virama*.)

Baybayin is of special interest here, though, for the same reason it interested these friar linguists: it offered an advantage when it came to writing the *saltillo* in Tagalog. Speakers of English can hear and produce a glottal stop easily between vowels, but these friar linguists had to learn to hear and utter it in more difficult combinations of Tagalog sounds: at the beginning of one syllable, and immediately after a consonant ending a previous syllable. So for instance they had to be able to hear and produce words which differed in the presence or absence of a glottal stop: *gab?i*, for instance, means "night," and it is just the use of a *saltillo* which differentiates it from *gabi*, which means "taro."

Friar linguists were at pains to master these kinds of differences, and for this reason found that they had special uses for *baybayin*'s three other symbols, which each represent a glottal stop followed by a different vowel. The symbol ꞊, for instance, can be transliterated as *?i*. Franciso de San José took advantage of this fact when he wrote his 1610 grammar of Tagalog, *Arte y reglas de la lengua Tagala*. In that work we find him using this *baybayin* character in an otherwise alphabetic, Castilian description of Tagalog to make clear differences in pronunciation. He did this by first writing words in *baybayin*, and then alphabetically. So *gab?i*, the word meaning "night" noted above, he wrote first as ꞊, which would be transliterated as *ga* () followed by *?i* (꞊). Then he wrote the second word as ꞊, showing afterwards that this corresponded to *ga* () and *bi* ().[4]

This is a tiny teaspoon drawn from the ocean of descriptive detail which can be a trial to read, but it helps to illustrate two points about this painstaking work. First, it suggests that friar linguists were willing and able to adapt their own habits of speech and practices of literacy in order to capture fine-grained properties of alien languages which they were, in fact, capable of recognizing. Second, it demonstrates how missions of faith engendered both a sense of care and a felt need for mastery over masses of such empirical details, to be gained by converting talk into inspectable writing. Even the humble *saltillo* had to be given its place in their larger projects of conversion.

Tracing links between these descriptive details and zones of contact involves broader aspects of the times and places where this work was done. So I consider next reasons for Carochi's larger concern with the "barbarism" of the misplaced *saltillo*, and then a question about *baybayin*: if friar linguists found it useful and "improvable," why did it eventually pass out of use among missionaries and native Tagalog speakers alike?

Civilized Illiterates

I cited Carochi's cautionary remark about the proper use of the *saltillo* earlier to illustrate a kind of political and cultural paradox: the Nahuatl were illiterate pagans who spoke a civilized language. This was one aspect of the larger social situation in which Carochi and other missionaries' strategies of descriptive selection and simplification served their broader work of conversion.

The Conquistadors realized early on that Mexico's and Peru's peoples were not like the "primitives" Columbus encountered in the Caribbean. Cortez likened cities he found in Mexico to Seville and Cordoba, and was as quick as Pizarro in Peru to see that power was to be had by usurping the native elite. He did this quite literally by murdering the king of the Mexican Indians, razing his palace, and building his own capital on its grounds.

In colonial era accounts of precolonical Mexico, the Aztec cult of human sacrifice often overshadow the sophisticated tributary systems used by noble elites to rule communities spread across a wide territory. Drawing members of subordinate, regional chieftainships to their royal centers of power was one way dominant elites could "culturally assimilate ... [them] to the ruling group ... [while] at the same time [they] served as hostage" (Carrasco 1982:35).

This political strategy supported parallel linguistic and social hierarchies: fluency in Nahuatl was a mark of proximity to, or membership in, high ranking social circles. Spoken by knowledgeable elites across more territory and in more situations than any local, provincial language, Nahuatl (like Quechua in Peru) was recognized by the Spaniards as what they called the *lengua general* of Mexico: a "principal intermediary language"[5] or, to use a more recent phrase I discuss in chapter 6, a "language of wider communication."

Just as different dialects of Nahuatl were spoken in different strata of Mexican society, so too different styles of Nahuatl were used by members of different groups more or less correctly, and more or less appropriately. Membership in the traditional elite was indirectly but powerfully marked by mastery of distinctively elaborate, allusive, prestigious genres of "lordly speech" (*tecpillatolli*), achieved only through long years of training and memorization. Fluency in this finely wrought language of poetry, oration, and ritual was thus a privilege and badge of those at the apex of an "extremely hierarchical society, in which an unbridgeable gap separated religious instruction for the rich and that for the poor" (de Alva 1982:349).

These social and linguistic hierarchies gave friar linguists strong reasons for focusing on one very specific dialect and style of Nahuatl to overcome two obstacles to their own purposes. First, to overcome problems of linguistic diversity in different locales of their work of conversion, they selected the dialect which was known in the largest number of places, contexts, and communities. Nahuatl was the natural candidate for such a *lengua general*. Second, they sought a style of Nahuatl which supported the high seriousness of their sacred purpose, hearing in "lordly speech" an echo of the authority of the true Faith: "[i]f the friars could usurp the power of those words, replacing the authority of the Indian past with that of Christianity, they would gain a significant degree of control over Indian thought and behavior, with all the social and political consequences that such control implies" (Burkhart 1989:11).

To convert Nahuatl into a lesser, written likeness of their own language of authority, missionaries' work of linguistic description was done in close parallel with the work of textual translation of native-language breviaries and confessional guides (Kartunnen 1982:396). This is one part of the backdrop for reading Carochi's warnings against misuse of the *saltillo*, a "barbarism" not just for those who are "very expert in the language" but in religious discourse designed to partake of the authority of "lordly speech." This work was descriptive and alphabetical, but also textual and rhetorical, as friars sought to devise genres of speech for addressing audiences of potential converts. But though they understood that reducing Nahuatl words to writing remade them in the image of Castilian, and as a surrogate for their own Truth language, they could not fully recognize that this did not give them ownership of the meanings of their Nahuatal oratory in the ears of Mexican audiences.

They intended to bring Nahuatl words, and the ideas they could express, into closer alignment with the reality of God's world. But they could not simply remove or displace those words' meanings as they already existed in Nahautl contexts, minds, or hearts. Rather, they produced a distinct new kind of discourse which became one among others. So, for instance, missionaries needed to explain their war against the Evil One, the *Diablo* or *demonio*, who had to be named in the Nahuatl language. To this end they took over the word *tlacatecolot* with the idea that it would be understood as were the Spanish words it translated. Missionaries had to ignore or imagine that they had simply displaced prior meanings of the Nahuatl language, in Nahuatl communities. In practice the missionaries did not so much bring awareness of the Evil One to their new flocks as introduce to them one more resident of the complex realm of spirits they knew to be populated by *tlacatecolot*, beings much more intimately and quite differently involved in Nahuatl lives than the Fallen Angel.

To designate the Eucharist, missionaries similarly devised a descriptive phrase with none of the original Latin's associations with a deep ritual past: speaking of the "white tortilla" conveyed no sense of the sacredness of the body of Christ it names, nor did the phrase which took its place, "divine white tortilla." Neither designation could convey the original's authority. Missionaries might have believed that with their practices of literacy they could improve the Nahuatl language along with the lives of their converts by revealing the real nature of the world. But they produced instead the distinctive new style David Tavárez (2000:23) describes as "doctrinal Nahuatl," a way of speaking associated with missionaries. This new style could not "silence indigenous voices, . . . resolve dialogue into monologue, [and] replace cultural diversity with conformity" (Burkart 1989:9). So the friars' work of conversion was lovingly destructive in a way they could not really afford to acknowledge: they could appropriate and deform Nahuatl into a written language of Christianity only by deforming the message of Christianity in ways they could not fully grasp.

Literate Primitives

I mentioned earlier that in the Philippines, friar linguists like de San José saw that *baybayin* was in some ways more useful than Latin, at least when it came to the problem of writing Tagalog's *saltillo*. Given this close, joined engagement with Tagalog writing and speech, why did *baybayin* eventually fall out of use? What in Tagalog life led missionaries to finally judge it incompatible with their larger purposes, so that it eventually passed from use? A bit of historical background helps to frame this question.

Cortez dispatched explorers from Mexico's west coast in 1528 in a continuing search for the Spice Islands. As emissaries of an emperor, Charles V, they carried letters he signed "Caesar Augustus, king of the Spains." Their voyage set in motion very different colonial developments in what now counts as island Southeast Asia, including those islands which were named the Philippines in 1541 in honor of Spain's heir apparent, Philip II.

At first those islands were a consolation prize and base of operations for the Spanish as they waited for an opportunity to displace Portugal from the real prize, the Spice Islands, to the south. A real irony of colonial history is that the Philippines were still a profitable possession for the Spanish centuries centuries after Portugal lost control of the Spice Islands to the Dutch. The Spanish reaped enormous profits from the trans-Pacific trade which met in Manila, the "pearl of the Orient," on the island of Luzon. Up through 1815, silver carried west from the New World was traded there for manufactured goods from China.

Because Spain's colonial interests became centered on trade and Manila, their dealings with "natives" beyond the town's environs did not become as intense or exploitative as those of their compatriots in the New World. Fewer Spanish ventured abroad to the new

colony, and oversight of the native populations and their souls was
left to the Church, represented by a clerisy which by 1722 was more
numerous in Manila than the lay population. Thanks to relatively
weak lines of colonial contact, the Philippines' natives were spared
many of the devastating diseases, forced labor, and wars of conquest which befell *los indios* in the New World.

On Luzon, the Spanish found little they counted as civilization:
local elites, such as they were, exercised limited authority over few
people and small expanses of territory; explorers found little silver
or gold – always a Spanish fixation – or other forms of wealth aside
from land, which was generally considered a communal resource;
there were no large "temples" and few settlements of any size away
from the coasts or in the inaccessible volcanic interior. Against this
"primitive" backdrop, writing systems like *baybayin* must have
seemed all the more peculiar.

Beyond any "defects" which friar linguists found in *baybayin*, two
other reasons can be offered for its demise. On one hand broad
shifts in political power and religious practice emanated from
Europe to the Philippines and elsewhere in the colonial world. On
the other, friars identified limitations not just in *baybayin* orthography, but in Tagalog practices of literacy it served.

In the second half of the 16th century the Church consolidated
its doctrinal foundation in reaction to the Reformation, and deci-
sions taken by the Council of Trent, beginning in 1545, gave new
grounds for caution among missionaries about deviating from religious orthodoxy (a wariness which might have been augmented by
missionaries' experiences in Mexico). New concerns arose about the
failure of translation, and the need to "safeguard the key words of
the doctrine from confusion with native beliefs and terminologies"
(Rafael 1993:117). Missionaries had learned that pagan words might
not be easily disentangled from pagan worlds.

For missionaries to introduce more words of Spanish and Latin
into their religious discourse for native converts, they had to introduce foreign speech sounds into native languages. Tagalog could
under those conditions be said to "lack" speech sounds like *r*, *z*, *f*,
v, and *f*, which are common in many Spanish and Latin words. For
missionaries who wrote these words, and required symbols for
sounds lacking in *baybayin*, that orthography came not just be
different from but deficient in relation to the alphabet.

Rafael (1993:53) also suggests that beyond *baybayin*'s orthographic indeterminacies, sketched above, missionaries resisted its use for a deeper reason: their inability to tolerate the gaps of meaning which could be created by the orthographic "gaps" mentioned above. These indeterminacies, Rafael suggests, marked a willingness to allow readings which passed "over sense in favor of sensation," and in that way ran directly against the grain of the missionaries' own "totalizing signifying practices." In this way the internal logic of *baybayin* posed a threat to the practices of literacy which grounded their sacred traditions of textual transmission.

But the existence of such an aesthetic of indeterminacy would not account for the fact that missionaries recognized ways to "improve" *baybayin*, rather than dispense with it. And it would seem peculiar that missionaries familiar with Hebrew writing, which incorporates many more such orthographic indeterminacies, touched on in chapter 3, would refuse to countenance those in *baybayin* which are, in the larger scheme of things, more limited.

One way to recast Rafael's insight is to consider *baybayin* orthographic conventions as they figured in the broader practices of literacy shared and transmitted among its users. In this respect the complaint of one missionary quoted earlier – that *baybayin* is "as easy to write as it is difficult to read" – is telling because it identifies a basic asymmetry between practices of writing and reading *baybayin*.

What Rafael calls the friars' "totalizing signifying practices" key to the one letter/one sound principle is mentioned in chapter 1. This enables a kind of symmetry between acts of reading and writing: knowledge of orthographic conventions is necessary and sufficient, at least in principle, to voice a text. But conventions of spelling need not require this symmetry, as a few exceptional spellings of English words help to demonstrate. When the letter *a* appears in the sequence of letters b-a-s-s, for instance, it has two possible pronunciations, rhyming with *pace* or *pass*, and can help to convey two different meanings. Ordinarily collateral information about the context of use will make this a trivial matter, although it is possible, in a written sentence like "That's a big bass," for that ambiguity to go unresolved. Only if reader and writer share knowledge of context and intention is it a trivial matter to disambiguate such spellings and meanings.

This example illustrates a general norm by violating it: texts are read with alphabetic practices of literacy as autonomous bearers of meaning. As an overriding ideal this is made very clear by Walter Ong, a modern Jesuit inheritor of the faith of the friar linguists I have discussed here. He celebrates the alphabet as a special means for

> abstractly analyzing the elusive world of sound into visual equiva-
> lents which sets [it] apart from other orthographies still very much
> immersed in the non-textual human life-world. (Ong 1977:90)

In chapter 3, I return to the broader meanings and uses of Ong's implicit parallel between the alphabet and "other orthographies" on the one hand, and those whose practices of literacy are less or more "immersed in the non-textual life-world" on the other.

It is significant in this regard that Europeans who encountered *baybayin* in wide use could find nowhere any significant body of written texts: "[t]hey have neither books nor histories nor do they write anything of any length but only letters and reminders to one another ... [lovers] carry written charms with them" (quoted in Scott 1994:210). They sought texts which were not just "longer" and more permanent than "letters" or "reminders," but which fit Ong's description better. "Letters" or "reminders" can be written on the presumption of knowledge shared by the writer and intended reader (topic, purpose, relevant history, etc.). A shopping list, for instance, can be all but indecipherable to someone who did not write it.[6]

Where alphabetic practices of literacy were bound to genres of historical writing and verbal art, those of *babayin* were not. For Tagalogs, poetry and literature were celebrated and appreciated in oral performance:

> The noblest literary form was the *siday* or *kandu*. This was the most
> difficult of all – long, sustained, repetitious, and heavy with meta-
> phor and allusion. A single one might take six hours to sing or the
> whole night through, or even continued the next night, during which
> rapt audiences neither yawned nor nodded, though the frequent
> repetition of long lines with only the variation of a few words struck
> Spanish listeners as tiresome. (Quoted in Scott 1994:98)

All of this suggests, then, that although missionaries could recognize *baybayin* as an *orthography* which was adequate for writing Tagalog speech sounds, they found later that it served no practices of literacy they judged adequate to their purposes. When practices of literacy appeared not just different but deficient in their situated, occasion-bound nature, *baybayin* came to be seen as an attribute of people who were literate but also primitive, and fell into that class of things which were to be studied "on the grounds of facilitating their eradication" (Burkhart 1989:3).

The Work of Loving Destruction

The work Ricard called "spiritual conquest" was done by creating hierarchical relations between humans with and through their languages. To appropriate pagan tongues, linguists reformed and deformed them with practices of literacy which let them remove words and meanings from native speech and speakers, before "giving them back" in their own religious discourses, and as symbols of their authority. These intimate and powerful relations could be created and sustained as long as natives' tongues were recognized as necessary but imperfect vessels of Christ's message.

But as friar linguists' early engagements with the *saltillo* show, their relations with those languages were fine-grained and empirical; Christian love drove them to observe, compare, and generalize, reducing textures of talk as fine and fleeting as the glottal stop to writing. This ability has always grounded missionaries' "mastery" of alien languages, and literacy has always lent authority to projects of conversion whose effects, as we will see in later chapters, always outran their intentions.

In Mexico, missionaries recognized hierarchies of language and class which conformed to their own social imaginaries, and which helped them to introduce literacy as the supplement needed to elevate lordly Nahuatl language as a means of spreading the Faith and converting its speakers. They undertook the work Patricia Seed (1991:13) calls "conquering language with language" on the presupposition that that they could bring Nahuatl into alignment with truth unilaterally, by making it their descriptive object.

Missionaries had difficulty recognizing, then, that they could only do the work of description and translation on what Dennis Tedlock (1983:334) calls the "dialogical frontier," and in larger colonial dynamics of accommodation and resistance, understanding and misunderstanding. So too the meanings of words shifted and slipped across colonial, religious, and linguistic divides as Nahuatl was deformed in writing, and Christian doxa was deformed in missionary discourse. Over time this dialogical process cumulatively affected language form and meaning alike so that, as Louise Burkhart (1989) puts it, the missionizers were themselves missionized.[7] Their founding faith and Walter Ong's assertion notwithstanding, their texts were never autonomous, or separable from life-worlds of friars or their flocks.

In the Philippines, successors to the friar linguists I have discussed retreated from these early intimate engagements with Tagalog, and became content to convey Christian doxa in a Spanish language few Tagalogs understood. Catholic identities became more firmly grounded in communities of religious practice, and less in discourse, as gulfs between priestly authority and colonial subjects opened up in ways acidly portrayed by Jose Rizal, an early Philippine nationalist, in his brilliant 1887 novel *Noli me tangere*.

This chapter's epigram is drawn from a parable for the success and failure of these friar linguists. Erdrich puts this observation about loving destruction in the mouth of a hero/ine, who speaks to his/her work as a priest in a community of native North Americans. Born a woman driven by the love of God, she lovingly destroyed her own gender to become a priest who could bring faith to others. This is a more physical image of loving destruction than the work of conversion I have described here, but it does echo transformations which Christian doxa had to undergo in Nahuatl and Tagalog letters, no matter how carefully friar linguists described and understood Nahuatl and Tagalog talk. However closely they listened, these first linguists could never fully reduce either to writing, or save the message they brought to destroy pagan ways of life.

Notes to chapter 2

1   In addition to extensive discussion of these traditions in Mignolo, see also articles in Boone and Mignolo (1994). A convenient

introduction to Mayan epigraphic traditions is given by Coe and Van Stone (2001).

2   The glottal stop is less obvious but common in casual American English as an alternant of *t* in pronunciations of words like "can't," "Latin," "written," and others where *t* would otherwise appear in close proximity with *n*.

3   If speakers of Philippine languages adapted scripts from their Buginese neighbors to the south, then there is a historical explanation for the fact that *baybayin* has no symbols for representing consonants when they close syllables: Buginese has almost no such syllables, and so no need to transcribe them.

4   Furthermore, he brought Latin letters it into better alignment with Tagalog speech by stipulating that he would use the letter *y* – which he didn't need for any other Tagalog speech sound – as an equivalent of *ʔi*, that is, glottal stop followed by *i*, represented in *baybayin* by ⇌. This allowed him to showing in alphabetic writing the difference between *gaby* (what I can write here as *gabʔi*) and *gabi*.

5   For discussion of Quechua's similar position among the Incas see John Rowe's (1982) discussion of similar Inca policies and institutions relating to the cultural unification of the empire.

6   So too Spanish accounts are unanimous in saying that Filipinos did not use their "alphabet" for record keeping, a practice which by its nature requires stable, unambiguous letter/sound and sign/meaning relations. This incompatability between practices of literacy became especially glaring when *baybayin* orthography was introduced into the colonial (and more generally Western) practices of literacy involved with documents like land transfers. These depend for their usefulness on readability at a remove, spatial and temporal, from the acts they record. Two such documents were written in *baybayin* in the late 16th century but, as Rafael describes it (1993:49), were readable by an archivist in the mid-20th century only with the aid of alphabetic documents which had been written by a contemporary Spanish notary.

7   For more on these dynamics see Lockhart 1991, 1992 and Hanks 2000 for discussions of literacy practices among Mayans of the Yucatan peninsula.

Chapter 3

Imaging the Linguistic Past

Who placed us with eyes between a microscopic and telescopic world?
Henry David Thoreau, *The journal of Henry D. Thoreau* (1962(6):133)

By the middle of the 18th century, microscopic accounts of alien languages like Nahuatl and Tagalog, written by missionaries, explorers, and others, were circulating back to Europe. Each fine-grained, highly circumscribed image of distant lives became part of the growing evidence that linguistic and human diversity far exceeded that previously imagined in Europe. Projects of exploration and exploitation at far-flung peripheries of the world were creating severe challenges for received ideas about human nature and history at home.

This chapter is about some important, early engagements with larger questions raised by this new knowledge of linguistic diversity, and new, telescopic views of the human past which began to develop in response. First I summarize speculative ideas of the German philosopher Johann Herder, and discoveries of the British philologist and colonial official William "Oriental" Jones, which were important in different ways for language-centered images of the deep human past in a 19th century science of language. Then I discuss some of the assumptions and purposes which informed these authors' two projects, showing how they gave new life to older social imaginaries of language and human history. It is important here to foreground overlapping images of the histories of texts and languages which helped make the science of language a way of legislating human differences in a rapidly colonializing world.

Herder's early, famous essay on language origins and diversity is too speculative to count as a foundation for any science, but it framed questions of human origins and identity in ideologically powerful ways. He offered compelling answers to pressing questions about language and human nature, and intellectual resources for two different kinds of projects: asserting colonial authority abroad, and creating national communities at home.

William "Oriental" Jones is a founding figure in linguistics thanks to studies in India, which led him to recognize resemblances between Sanskrit on one hand, and Greek, Latin, and languages of modern Europe on the other. But Jones' studies as a "philologer" were in service to his primary duties as a judge working for the British East India Company in Bengal. His joined projects of (linguistic) knowledge and (colonial) authority made him famous as "Oriental" Jones, an emblematic figure in the intellectual tradition which came to be known as orientalism.

Important here are the ways Herder and Jones blurred lines between what now seem very different kinds of histories: of *written texts* on one hand and *language systems* on the other. These overlaps helped give new life to old biblical images of the past, renewing what Trautmann (1997) calls "Mosaic ethnology." New telescopic visions of language change and diversity helped to "reconstitute, redeploy, and redistribute old religious patterns of human history and destiny" (Said 1994:121). To show how these two new images of the linguistic past could legitimize European authority abroad, I conclude this chapter with a sketch of two different versions of Javanese history, allowing otherwise different stories about its literature and language to prove, in correspondingly different ways, the inferiority of Javanese in a colonial present.

Herder's Story of Language Origins

Johann Herder (1744–1803) stepped onto the European intellectual stage as Immanuel Kant's greatest student, and became a famous public intellectual whose voluminous writings helped to "open philosophy out onto the world." Most famous among his writings, though, is his early essay submitted for a contest sponsored by the Berlin Academy of Science in 1769. The academy's question, posed in French, was whether "men, left to their natural faculties, [are] in a position to invent language, and by what means do they, by themselves, accomplish that invention." Herder's victory in this contest marked this expatriate school teacher's rapid ascent into the elite of German-speaking society, a figure who would cast a shadow over generations of political philosophers, educators, philologists, and others.

The prize question was hardly novel. It had been the subject of longstanding debate, particularly among leading French thinkers whose positions had become widely known in European intellectual circles. Hans Aarsleff, a historian of linguistics, argues that there was little new in Herder's essay (Aarsleff 1982). But besides considerably simplifying Herder's position and tracing his intellectual debts to influential French philosophers of the time, Aarsleff is concerned more with ideas speaking to ideas than an essayist addressing a particular audience. More important here are questions about this essay's influence and rhetorical force for its predominantly German readership.

Considering the sources of this essay's influence helps to read it as an answer to one question, about language, in order to address another, about identity and history. The more immediate question, posed by global linguistic and human diversity, had implications for Europeans' understandings of their place in a widening world. The other question, less direct and more local, was driven by a political and cultural crisis confronting Germans (or speakers of German): an encroaching French state and civilization. France's intellectual and political ascendance over the Holy Roman Empire – where Germans lived as subjects of a fractured nobility, on patchworks of landholdings – was evident in the very fact that the Berlin Academy posed this question in French. I discuss these political and cultural issues in the next chapter, but mention them here as an aspect of the context in which Herder aimed to address his readers in a forceful, somewhat colloquial German, not just as a philosopher but a German writing for other Germans.

It is convenient here to summarize Herder's argument as having two parts. The first is about the coalescence of languages out of organic relations between humans and their environments; this is a story which denies divine intervention, and insists instead on the naturalness of linguistic sharedness and expressive authenticity. This became a foundational theme for romanticist philosophy and nationalism in following decades, a part of what Terry Eagleton calls Herder's "conscious assault on the universalism of the Enlightenment" (2000:12). For Eagleton, this also grounded Herder's protest against European colonial projects on behalf of those from "all the quarters of the globe who have not lived and perished for the dubious honour of having their posterity made happy by a speciously superior European culture" (2000:12).

The second part of Herder's essay, less well-known, extends this story of origins, arguing that languages have developmental trajectories which explain intrinsic inequalities between them and their speakers. This is important as a kind of prototype for the much more elaborate, influential accounts of linguistic and human history which developed over the next century, allowing telescopic constructions of global human difference to be based on specious comparisons of microscopic linguistic facts. Herder showed how to make "facts" of language history into proofs of human inequality; in this way he also demonstrated the darker side of linguistic and cultural relativism, as romanticism contributed to the sense of otherness of colonial subjects whose humanity could be counted as incommensurable with that of their masters.[1]

Herder begins his essay with a paradox: how is it that the human organism has physical senses which are so much weaker than those of many other species in the world, yet human communities – as explorers had amply demonstrated – are able to survive and thrive in so many more environments around the world than other species? The diversity of what we now call ecological niches in which human communities have places must be due, Herder argued, to some other distinctive human capacity, which became central to his explanation of language origins. The term he used for this capacity he borrowed from his teacher, Immanuel Kant. *Besonnenheit* might be translated into English as "reflection," but Herder describes it as a kind of synthetic, intuitive sense behind the physical senses, a capacity constantly engaged with and shaping experience as it flows through the senses from the world into bodies. *Besonnenheit* is what allows humans to abstract out or fix some elements of that flow, and so mediates between natural environments in which the body's senses are located, and internal experiences of those environments.

After arguing (none too plausibly) that hearing is privileged among the senses, Herder proceeds to trace the emergence of language from dynamic relations between *Besonnenheit* and auditory experience in particular locales. Thanks to their ability to bind small parts of the flow of auditory experience in time, humans can recognize that they resemble each other, and so also are bound to experiences of the environment. Once some patterns in the flow of auditory experience are recognized – the sound of a sheep bleating is Herder's example – they can be brought into reflective relation with experience of things in the world which produce them, and so understood to represent those things ("the bleater"). In this way the first words emerge, and with them language, from experience of the world. By appealing only to natural capacities of human organisms, Herder is able to explain language origins without any appeal to divine intervention.

Linguists, who nowadays refer to this as the "bow-wow" theory of language origins, distance themselves from what they regard as rank speculation. But Herder broadened his argument to frame language as both human and natural because it related "external and internal to one another reciprocally . . . There is no expression of the physical which does not immediately appear as 'spiritual,' as the symbol of some psychic process of reworking" (Pross quoted in Zammito 2002:324). By focusing on senses, environments, and experience, Herder downplayed the conventionality of language – its character as a kind of *sameness of knowledge* distributed among speakers – to foreground its experiential and expressive immediacy, grounding modes of *social sharedness*. Language joins bodies to each other in and through shared environments. A "place is sensed [when] senses are placed," and language helps "places make sense [when] senses make place" (Feld 1996:91).

Herder's story allows no firm line between nature and culture, or individual and community. Thought and expression combine in words and the "ocean of sensations" from which they emerge. This profoundly plural vision of "human nature" is grounded in what Charles Taylor calls, in his insightful discussion of Herder, the "linguistic dimension" of life: the "space of attention, of distance from the immediate instinctual significance of things" (Taylor 1995:88). As languages differ, so do "linguistic dimensions" of life.

One attractive point of Herder's essay was that it accounted for language origins and diversity in the same way, offering an alternative to the story of Babel. If *Besonnenheit* is a part of human nature, then linguistic diversity emerges as a natural consequence of experience of the diversity of environments in which it has operated. Languages and communities are natural outgrowths of diverse locales, which is one reason Herder was deeply suspicious of colonialism: it was a literally unnatural outside force or power which could only destroy any locale, language, and community, a "Trojan Horse . . . that seek[s] to subvert this naturally plural world" (Pagden 1995:144).

In his essay's second part, Herder shifts attention from language origins to language history, and develops a strategy of linguistic comparison to corroborate a broader argument based on linguistic "facts." This early framing of what would later become dominant organic images of linguistic and human difference keyed to the notion that languages, like all living things, partake of the cycle of birth, maturation, and death. Once this cycle is in motion, it sustains and is sustained in language and culture across generations of shorter lived human organisms, such that human collectives develop in one or another direction, and achieve a greater or lesser apex of maturity. Each language has a developmental dynamic of its own, like any living thing: "it sprouts, it blossoms, it flowers, and it withers – so it is with language" (Menze and Jenges 1992:104).

These organic trajectories, Herder argues, are evident in specific properties of exotic languages which, in his judgment, have moved past their highest stage of development into states of decadence or dormancy. Here his philosophical, telescopic point of view is joined to a presentation of microscopic details drawn from various linguistic descriptions. These provide what counted for him, and the linguists who followed him as ample evidence that languages around the world are either immature or moribund. They provide detailed evidence, in his view, of the rudimentary character of what he calls "unpolished" languages: Chinese, Siamese, the language of the Lapps, Quechua (spoken in the Andes), as well as that "outstandingly imperfect" language, Arabic (Herder 1966:154). That these languages exist is significant for Herder as important evidence against any argument for the divine origin of human languages: no divine being, he notes, would ever have created such imperfect things.

This "empirical" part of Herder's argument develops as demonstration, rather than speculation, through a wide series of parallel contrasts joining language structure, language use, and human communities. Words and word roots of unpolished languages, he argues, conform to sensual experience (i.e., are onomatopoeic) more than those of polished languages; unpolished languages show an "unnecessary abundance" of synonyms, unlike polished languages, but have less developed grammars; unpolished languages belong to communities of speakers who have (feminine) genres of song and poetry, unlike those whose polished languages make possible (masculine) genres of prose and philosophy.

Read with hindsight, these analogies seem at best to be evidence of ignorance or naiveté about facts and meanings of linguistic diversity. But in Herder's time and place the success of this argument testifies to the power of these language-based ideas about human difference, such that they could shape the 19th century science of language I describe in chapter 4.

Herder has a special place in his essay for literacy as the crucial point dividing languages (and peoples) who count as "unpolished" and "polished." This is because literacy is both an outcome and a sign of the workings of *Besonnenheit* which in turn becomes an instrument of *Besonnenheit*. So different literacies can be compared on the same universal metric of "polish," and Herder could establish the importance of Hebrew, a language which he studied throughout his life, in human development. Hebrew never crossed the crucial threshold to alphabetic writing, he argues, because its letters "are exclusively consonants [whereas] precisely those elements of the word on which everything depends, the self-sounding vowels, were originally not written at all" (Herder 1966:93). Why was Hebrew's development truncated? Because, in Herder's judgment, of the quality of spoken Hebrew's vowels: "they could not be written. Their pronunciation was so alive and finely articulated, their breath so spiritual and etherlike that it evaporated and eluded containment in letters. It was only with the Greeks that these living aspirations were pinned down in formal vowels" (Herder 1966:93).

Perhaps Herder had not read about Nahuatl as described by friar linguists in Mexico, or Tagalog in the Philippines; if he had perhaps he would not have argued that "[t]he more alive a language is the less too is it writeable" (Herder 1966:93). But as it happens he set out a position echoed much later by Walter Ong, whose reflections on alphabetic writing I mentioned in chapter 2. Herder and Ong both developed analogical differences between alphabetic and nonalphabetic orthographies on one hand, and mental abilities, arrayed along a developmental trajectory, on the other. Because they make language difference symptomatic of deeper differences between humans, they require only a short step from a relativist celebration of difference to a legitimizing explanation of inequality. Herder establishes a fundamental asymmetry between speakers of more polished languages (like Herder, and us) who can know and those who, as speakers of unpolished languages, are fated to be known.

Within Europe, this pluralistic vision inspired nationalist ideologies which I discuss in chapter 4, as it progressively forced "old sacred languages – Latin, Greek, and Hebrew . . . to mingle on equal ontological footing with a motley plebeian crowd of vernacular rivals" (Anderson 1991:70). But in the larger world, it combined with equally powerful images of the advancement of reason to explain the gulf between modern and primitive humans. It is important here that Herder did this by turning language on itself to establish his own position as inheritor and exponent of the civilizational dynamic. This double distancing of the modern from the primitive can be seen by locating his argument in a broader, mature definition of "civilization" which was formulated in 1930, at the height of the imperial age:

[linguistic diversity] is . . . a fact and . . . [Herder] studies it as such; he exercises his mind on facts; and when he discovers the general laws which govern the development and life of the world, even those laws are simply facts which he observes. And then the knowledge of external facts develops in [him and] us ideas which dominate these facts . . . as a spectator he is subject to facts; as an actor he remains

master in imposing upon them a more regular and a purer form.
(Febvre 1930:247)

Herder's self-positioning was implicit in his linguistic image of the
past, and later in the first science of language he inspired.

Imaging the Oriental Past

About the time Herder wrote his essay on language origins, William
"Oriental" Jones' studies of the Sanskrit language were coming to
the attention of educated Europeans. So important were Jones' discoveries that his Presidential address at the first meeting of the
Asiatic Society of Bengal, in 1786, is taken by many as foundational
for linguistics. So it is common for histories of the field to include
the following quotation:

> [T]he Sanscrit language, whatever be its antiquity, is of a wonderful
> structure; more perfect than the Greek, more copious than the Latin,
> and more exquisitely refined than either; yet bearing to both of them
> a stronger affinity . . . than could possibly have been produced by
> accident; so strong indeed that no philologer could examine them all
> three without believing them to have sprung from some common
> source, which, perhaps, no longer exists; there is a similar reason,
> though not quite so forcible, for supposing that both the Gothick and
> Celtick, though blended with a different idiom, had the same origin
> with the Sanscrit; and the old Persian might be added to the same
> family. (Quoted in Trautmann 1997:38)

Hindsight makes it is easy to find in this passage what Thomas
Trautmann (1997:39) calls a "precocious modernity:" an ability to
recognize the implications of new facts when take together with
others long known, and to reason from them all to a sweeping new
vision of the past.[2]

But as founding figure in the larger colonial enterprise of power
and knowledge, critiqued by Edward Said in his book *Orientalism*
(1994), "Oriental" Jones can also be regarded as having accomplished this feat because of the transparent relations between his
need for linguistic knowledge and political interests. Jones came to

the study of Sanskrit in the first place because he judged it necessary for his work as an officer of the East Indies Company responsible for administering justice to "the natives."

Said passed over Jones' linguistic work in *Orientalism* in favor of French studies of Semitic languages, but he surely knew that Jones' work answered his broad description of a "Western style for dominating, restructuring, and having an authority" (Said 1994:3). Jones answers well in this respect, at least, to Said's description of the orientalist as

> a hero rescuing the Orient from the obscurity, alienation, and strangeness which he himself had properly distinguished . . . having transported the Orient into modernity, the Orientalist could celebrate his method, and his position, as that of a secular creator, a man who made new worlds as God had once made the old. (Said 1994:121)

But Jones' "discoveries" and methods were not entirely new. Europeans, including other Britons, had been engaged with exotic Indian languages and literatures long before he studied them, and had produced grammars, dictionaries, and translations of the New Testament for speakers of the Tamil language, spoken further south on the subcontinent. Other Europeans had encountered Sanskrit long before Jones, noted the same correspondences with European languages which caught his attention, and speculated in the same vein about some ancient original source.[3]

Jones did his linguistic work in large part by extending traditions of etymological study already well known in Europe, which were being exported to other borders of European expansion. In Russia and the United States – just freed from one colonial project and embarking on its own conquests – word lists were circulating to gather information about aboriginal languages. These projects were inspired by Gottfried Leibniz, who had observed in the 17th century that comparison between languages – "the most ancient monuments of peoples" – could provide clues to the common origin of nations.

So Jones' discoveries had tremendous impact not just because they were novel, but because he had readers in the intellectual circles of Europe who were already "seething with curiosity" about languages of the Orient (Schwab 1984:23). He gave them texts which could be read for a fine-grained but telescopic view of historically distant objects, albeit within a highly delimited field of vision. Reading at a distance, they could extend the shared social imaginaries and habits of thought which made Jones' methods and conclusions plausible for them. They were ready to recognize, for one thing, that scholarly expertise which had been developed in the study of the history of *texts* could be transposed naturally to the study of the history of *languages*. This simple but important point has been discussed by a historian of linguistics, Henry Hoenigswald (1974), who pointed out how it was these two joined areas became subjects of different fields of study in the 19th century. Drawing on Hoenigswald's observations here, I foreground the ways Jones' image of "deep" linguistic and human history gained plausibility and power because from it extended ideas and images which now count as conceptually distinct.

Jones took to India a considerable reputation as a "philologer," that is, a student of exotic textual traditions who at age 33 "knew" a dozen languages: not just Latin, Greek, and Hebrew, but the more exotic Arabic, Turkish, and Persian, this last especially important as a language of power in India. Philologers had no need to be able to speak these languages, so long as they were versed in practices of literacy which allowed them to engage with texts written in those languages.

In 1783, after Jones left the scholarly life for the law, and traveled to Fort William in Calcutta, he took an appointment as judge for the British East India Company. He discovered, though, an unexpected but real need for his expertise as a philologer when consultations with native experts – "professors of the Hindu law," he called them – showed them to be insufficiently knowledgeable about their own textual traditions. In his view they neither understood nor applied their legal traditions consistently and correctly and so obliged Jones to study and master that tradition himself in order to gain direct access to original authoritative texts, and avoid "reliance . . . on [native] opinions or interpretation . . . examin[ing] their authorities and quotations, and detect[ing] their errors and misrepresentations" (quoted in Aarsleff 1983:119). Jones the philologer came to the aid of Jones the judge to make it an "impossibility for the Mohammedan or Hindu lawyers to impose upon us with erroneous opinions."

This work of textual excavation required Jones to obtain multiple versions of texts which, once gathered, could be compared with each other in great detail. Each had value, then, not in itself, but as one of a group, an instance of a category, and a more or less imperfect replica of the ultimate object of knowledge: the original, authoritative, but absent ur-text from which each was "descended." Here is a broad description of the goals and methods of this kind of reconstruction:

> The aim of this method is to construct a family-tree of MSS., called a stemma. At the top stands the archetype, the MS. from which all extant MSS. are derived. . . . If it can be shown that the surviving MSS. are traceable to several lost ancestors, intervening between the archetype and them, then these intermediate stages can be indicated with Greek letters, e.g., α and β . . . The value of the stemma is that it can show the genetic relation of MSS. And hence which are closer to what we are seeking. (Robson 1988:14)

I draw here from Stuart Robson's introduction to Dutch traditions of study of Javanese literature, which I discuss later, to foreground the basic images and metaphors which went into the work of reconstructing texts. Relations of "descent" between texts can be charted on "family trees" which link existing texts to their "ancestors" through "genetic relations." These biological metaphors combine and support a linguistic image of the past like that in Figure 3.1.

In this scheme, texts are objects (MS1, MS2, etc.) located at different distances in historical time (t_{n+1}, t_{n+2}, etc.) from a common, archetypal point of origin (t_n). To work out links between them is to deduce the properties of their common point of origin by comparing traits to establish the intervening acts of writing/copying which produced them. This way of reading makes texts' internal contours and coherence less important than their isolable traits, which can be identified and compared as individual facts. There is a circular logic at work here: relations between physical entities can be established by postulating that there exists some shared but absent ur-text; but that ur-text can only ever be known by studying its putative descendants.

Figure 3.1 also presents an image of history as a series of punctuated events, rather than cumulative development: texts result from

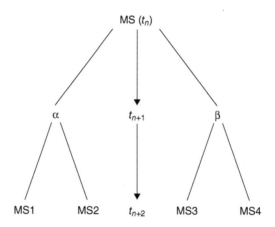

Figure 3.1   The philological image of textual descent.

events of writing in different times (and maybe spaces) which need to be brought into analytic proximity. The overall contour that connects these points, in turn, is a progressive distancing and falling away from a perfect, originary moment, because acts of copying introduce cumulatively more deviations.

Said argues that this kind of textual appropriation was ideologically important because it blurs the difference between senses of textual history on one hand, and social history on the other, Substituting the first for the second, as part for whole, helped to "convert . . . Indian forms of knowledge into European objects" (Cohn 1996b:21). Bernard Cohn, a critical historian of colonial India, suggests that Jones was able in this way to bring together two modalities of knowledge and power: as judge he operated in an investigative modality, gathering facts and reaching conclusions; as a philologer he operated in a historiographic modality, saving texts from the corrupting effects of time and larger processes of civilizational decay.

Said also recognized the self-authorizing grounds of civilizational advance in these methods. The application of reason could not only provide natives with their own languages in writing, as discussed in chapter 2, but could also give them back their textual legacy in a new era of knowledge and reason.

From Text to Language

Philologers worked to reconstruct original texts by studying their descendants as ensembles of instances of language use – words, roots, and grammatical elements – in the European tradition of etymological speculation. This was the study reputed to have been called by Voltaire "a science in which vowels count for nothing, and consonants for very little." Jones devoted considerable attention to the histories of particular words, but the logic of comparison and generalization which he demonstrated could be transposed to other dimensions of language, which I discuss in chapter 4.

To illustrate his etymological approach, I can sketch a single group of words: patterns of letters and meaning which can be drawn out of texts, and compared with each other to allow inferences about larger aggregates or ensembles of facts: the entire languages in which those texts (and perhaps indefinitely many others) were written. So words for "mother" can be abstracted from texts written thousands of miles and centuries apart, and listed together as Table 3.1.

Compared across texts and languages, such elements license broader inferences about where and when languages were spoken, and so about geographical and historical relations between groups or communities of speakers. The comparison of languages in this way allows much greater historical and geographical depth, which can be illustrated here by anticipating my sketch in chapter 4 of the comparative science of language which explored that "deep history." The culmination of this image of the linguistic past, devised in the 1860s, is the so-called Indo-European language tree (*Stammbaum* in German) shown in Figure 3.2.

I present this image here to emphasize its parallels and differences with the image of textual descent in Figure 3.1, which are easy to take for granted because both are grounded in biological metaphors of descent. Languages, like texts, are commonly spoken of as being related to each other like kin, as "parent" forms, which may no longer be extant, with "daughter" forms.

This is a convenient way of framing relations in time because it makes it easy to overlook differences between the dynamics and events which go into relations of "descent" mapped with these two

Table 3.1 Some Indo-European words for "mother".

Old Indic	*mātár-
Avestian	mātar-
Armenian	mair
Albanian	motrë
Latin	māter
Umbric	matrer
Lettisch	mate
Lithuanian	motera
Germanic	*mōthar
Dutch	moeter
Old Church Slavonic	mati
Old English	mōdor
Tocharian	mācar
Greek	mētēr
Low German	moder
Old High German	muoter
Old Saxon	môdar
Old Norse	móthorner
Swedish, Danish	moder
Old Teutonic	mōdar

Asterisks are used by philologists to mark forms of words not as they have been encountered in texts, but that have instead been reconstructed by comparative analysis of forms found in texts. This convention was introduced by August Schleicher, and is discussed in chapter 4.

figures. Figure 3.1 displays nodes which branch at points in the lives of individuals, copyists who produced different instances of texts; Figure 3.2 displays nodes which branch at points in the histories of communities as they moved in different directions or otherwise became separated. Texts are products of human agents; "daughter" languages emerge from "ancestor" languages by a kind of parthogenesis or fission in which individuals count as an anonymous, homogeneous substrate.

Because relations of descent among languages involve movements in space, and continuity between generations of speakers, the Indo-European tree in Figure 3.2 can be read as an image not just

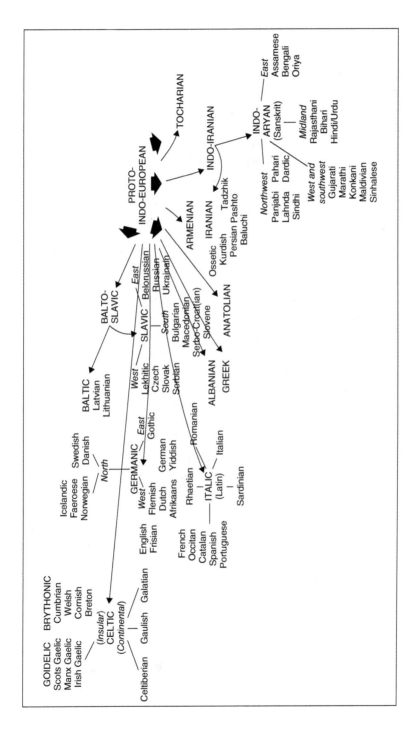

Figure 3.2 Indo-European or proto-Indo-European migrations in time and space. Redrawn from Crystal 1997. Reprinted by permission of Cambridge University Press.

of relations of "descent" in time, but of the movement of languages/ speakers in space (roughly speaking) from east to west (i.e., "right" to "left") and north to south (i.e., "top" to "bottom").

Jones' textual studies were predicated on the assumption that texts, once produced, could not somehow come back together or "merge," as might indeed happen should some copyist compare two older texts – in the manner of a philologer – to produce one not exactly like either. So too mappings of linguistic descent depend on the assumption that communities of speakers, once having become separate, remain so, such that their ways of speech do not influence each other.

"Oriental" Jones' broad vision of the deep linguistic past can also be seen as being grounded in another authoritative resource for thinking about deep history: the Old Testament. Jones was a man of reason but also faith, who saw in India's textual traditions a resource for arriving at a clearer understanding of biblical narratives of the origins of the world and humanity, and correcting errors introduced into copied and recopied versions of the original, true story of Genesis. Thomas Trautmann has pointed out that Protestant faith grounded Jones' work, and led him to emulate his hero Isaac Newton, who similarly sought to correct biblical chronology with his astronomical expertise, fine-tuning calculations of the exact date of the creation of the world proposed by Bishop Usher.[4] So, too, Jones saw in exotic texts and linguistic diversity a key to the location of the tower of Babel, and a way of recovering the language spoken when Adam and Eve were cast out from the garden of Eden.

Trautmann describes Jones' view of the biblical past as being grounded in a "Mosaic ethnology," and an image of the human past grounded in lines of patrilineal descent: lists of names of men connected by a series of "begats." This is a kind of descent which is called unilineal, because it allows for a reckoning of human relatedness across generations through just one parental line. By naming links between fathers/sons, but not mothers with children of either gender, patrilineal descent makes for a bracketing of parts of the biological givens of human "descent." Familiar images of the deep past, transposed to previously unknown circumstances, helped to create a new framework of knowledge when "language" came to name a group of objects which were similarly located and related in time and space.

Two Stories about Sanskrit and Javanese

Texts, grammars, and genealogies can all be represented with the broad historical image I have outlined here without discussing any particular colonial project. To show its importance as a resource for legitimizing colonial authority, I can conclude this chapter by comparing two different ways this image figured in the study of the literature and grammar of a single language, Javanese. These accounts are worth sketching to show that this image helped to create pictures of that language's past which were in important ways contradictory, but which nonetheless both helped to explain Javanese speakers' inferiority to the Dutch (among other Europeans) who came to rule them in a 19th century colonial regime.

I noted in chapter 2 that the Sanskrit language which Jones "discovered" was in its own way as well traveled as Latin, but not as a language of power imposed by conquerors on their subjects (Pollock 2000). As Sanskrit traveled with traders, religious professionals, and literati it was assimilated into local languages and societies. In much of Asia, Europeans encountered orthographies they came to recognize as similar to Sanskrit, and literary traditions eight hundred or a thousand years old. Long periods of time had allowed for dynamic interplay between Indic literature and local languages, producing the "vernacular" literary cultures, as Pollock calls them, which Europeans discovered and studied.

Java offered clear evidence of extensive influence from India in the deep past: Hindu (Sivite) and Buddhist temples, and an extensive body of literature written in what was once called the Kawi language, and is now more frequently called Old Javanese. Dutch colonialists paid little attention to this literature until the beginning of the 19th century, when their interests shifted from trade with the Spice Islands to control of the kingdoms of inland Java, whose ruling nobility had inherited Kawi texts as a legacy from their pre-Islamic past.

The British occupied Java during the Napoleonic Wars, and so between 1812 and 1814 Kawi came to the attention of governor Stamford Raffles (who owes his fame more to his founding of Singapore). His compendious *History of Java* (1979[1817]) drew the attention of European readers to this ancient Javanese language, including Wilhelm von Humboldt, a founding figure in German philology, whom I discuss in the next chapter.

Von Humboldt took steps to acquire unpublished Kawi texts because he regarded that language as a test case for the broad ideas about language, culture, and history which were then developing in German intellectual circles – which included Johann Herder. Von Humboldt saw in Kawi texts the possibility of establishing whether (as Herder argued) languages are in fact organically bound to environments and communities of speakers, and so "naturally" resistant to influences from "outside." Kawi was interesting in this regard because it was originally a "primitive" language, ordinary Javanese, which had come under the influence of polished, written Sanskrit. Kawi literature was where "Indian influence was most deeply and penetratingly at work upon Malayan (i.e., Javanese) culture" and so, von Humboldt believed, should bear clearest evidence of "the most intimate intertwining of Indian and indigenous culture . . . on the island that possessed the earliest and most numerous Indonesian settlements" (von Humboldt 1988[1836]:20).

Von Humboldt explored this question in what became a sprawling, famous, but now largely unread four-volume opus: *On the Kawi language.* In this work von Humboldt sifted lexical material (as did Jones) for evidence of "genetic" relations, discovering them between Javanese and languages spoken as far north as Luzon, as far east as the South Sea islands, and Madagascar to the west. (In this way he charted the largest dimensions of another of the world's major language families, now called Austronesian.)

But von Humboldt's focus was Kawi grammar, which led him to study the oldest available Javanese version of the Sanskrit epic *Bharata Yuddha.* He appreciated this text aesthetically, as a "literary monument" from the past, but sought to read it diagnostically for the data that would speak to larger questions about language and human history. His basic conclusion was that "however many Sanskrit words it may have incorporated, [Kawi] does not cease on that account to be a Malayan tongue." In fact, "it robbed the incomparably nobler Sanscrit of its own form, to force it into the local one" (von Humboldt 1988[1836]:33).

Von Humboldt developed a language-centered story about a primitive people who were incapable of fully incorporating the benefits of an "outside" civilization, one with a larger moral for those concerned with contemporary questions about civilizational expansion and colonial power. If Java had never been home to more than a kind of civilization *manqué*, then Europeans there were dealing now with modern inheritors of a lesser tradition whose ancestors had fallen away from a civilization they never really made their own. In this way they differed from Europeans, von Humboldt noted, whose ancestors had taken up the language of Rome's imperial project with a new vigor and liveliness.

Another, very different, text-centered picture of Java's past coalesced in another body of work by Dutch scholars. By 1830, the Dutch had supremacy in Java after defeating Prince Dipanegara, whose revolution in the name of Islam gave them one more reason to fear and distrust that religion: its monotheistic theology strengthened native resistance to Christianity, and had the potential to transform docile peasants into revolutionary fanatics. As they consolidated control of the interior of Java, and increased their contact with its noble houses, the Dutch became more aware of the rich body of literary Javanese texts, and began the work of textual comparison and reconstruction I noted above. Over the decades, scholars produced critical editions and translations of a range of works of Javanese literature written as early as 1000 CE, and as recently as the 18th century.

Taken as a whole, and simplifying greatly, the overarching historical narrative which came to be told about this body of work can be seen as resonating with that developed by Jones and other British scholars for India. It told of the decay of an ancient Sanskritic tradition that fell away from its original, pure beauty. The commonest periodizing of this literature – Old, Middle, and Modern Javanese – implicitly makes Old Javanese a reference point for evaluating the fidelity of later texts to the original, "correct" Sanskrit vocabulary, quotations, and glosses of verses. This narrative also fits Said's profile for the orientalist scholar as bringer of European reason to recuperate and restore traditions for their native inheritors.

In Java, at least, this way of elevating an older, more "authentic" past had broader political significance in an Islamic present. Islam in this narrative was a latecomer to the island, arriving no earlier than the 15th century, and putting a "thin varnish of Mohammadanism over a base of Buddhism and Saivism" (Florida 1995:188).

The textual scholars who recovered that "base" for the Javanese could in this way help save them from the "gullibility and ignorance . . . [which made them] easy prey for those who, under mask of religion (i.e., Islam), hide sinister intents" (Florida 1995:188).

In this way, then, grammar-centered and text-centered versions of Javanese history could differ in substance but legitimize both European superiority in the world, and Dutch rule in Java. Von Humboldt compared lexical and grammatical elements to understand "large-scale" historical connections between peoples, whereas Dutch philologists compared texts within a single historical tradition to deduce links of "descent" (and decay) between them. Where von Humboldt demonstrated the imperviousness of a primitive language to the benefits of its civilized superior, the Dutch traced the decay of an ideal language rooted in that same civilized language, and showed how that decay was being hastened if not caused by the incursions of a false religion. Two language-centered images of the past, guided and shaped by social imaginaries and scholarly procedures, helped develop multiple understandings of Europeans' place, obligations, and privileges in a colonizing world.

The Linguistic Past in the Colonial Present

The linguistic images of the past I have sketched here came into full maturity in the science of language, comparative philology, which I discuss in the next chapter. There I trace images of linguistic descent-as-reproduction, which in turn were exported to the colonialized world as an important aid for Europeans who made languages and language difference go hand in hand "with the creation and reification of social groups . . . [on a] social and political map" (Cohn 1996b:22).

I have focused here on comparative philology's prehistory to show how microscopic, recondite linguistic details could figure in broader questions about global human diversity, and telescopic views of alien, colonialized peoples. William Jones may have been constructing a "rational defense of the Bible out of the materials collected by Orientalist scholarship" (Trautmann 1997:42), but the historical contours of his defense could be transposed and adapted to many other contexts and purposes. Shared social imaginaries helped make the story that Jones and other philologists developed the best sort, which, as Winston Smith notes in *1984*, we already know.

Herder was a speculative philosopher but no linguist, and his framing of linguistic diversity was more speculative than empirical, and explicitly nonbiblical. But his was a story of destinations pregiven with origins, and carried its own legitimizing moral for Europe's nations in the world they were beginning to dominate. He showed Germans, and other Europeans, that with their own languages they inherited their futures, each what the linguist von Humboldt called an "emanation of the spirit, no work of nations but a gift fallen to them by their inner destiny" (von Humboldt 1988[1836]:24).

Notwithstanding differences between their images of the linguistic past, Herder and Jones together helped to frame a scholarly and colonial project which would "transmute polyglot agonies of Babel into a cult of transcendent European erudition" (Herzfeld 1987:31). From their painstaking microscopic studies emerged a telescopic view of linguistic and human diversity as "a marvelous, almost symphonic whole whose progress and formations, again as a whole, could be studied exclusively as a concerted and secular historical experience, not as an exemplification of the divine" (Said 1995:21).

Notes to chapter 3

1   For further discussion of this issue from an anthropological point of view, see Johannes Fabian's *Time and the other* (1983).
2   For extensive discussion of scholars who prepared the ground for Jones' famous work on one hand, and Herder's influential philosophy on the other, see Aarsleff 1983 and Trautmann 2006.
3   See for instance Metcalf 1974 and Gulya 1974.
4   Bishop Ussher had calculated that the world was created in 4004 BC, and that God caused the flood of Noah in 2349 BC.

Chapter 4

Philology's Evolutions

[T]his crowd has thrown itself into the science of language: here, in an endless region of tillable land, freshly opened up, where presently even the most mediocre gifts can be employed with profit and a certain emptiness is already even considered as a positive talent, with the newness and insecurity of the methods and the continuous danger of fantastical errors.

Friedrich Nietzsche, *On the future of our educational institutions* (2004[1872]:71)

Nietzsche may have had more respect for leading figures in the "science of language" than members of the crowd whose imaginations, as he observed in the passage above, the new field had seized. By the time he made this remark, in a lecture on Prussia's educational institutions, that science – *Sprachwissenschaft*, or comparative philology – had come fully into its own due to new discoveries and insights into "deep" historical relations among languages and humankind. He might have been skeptical rather of comparative philology's ascendance over his own field, text-centered, classical philology (*Alterthumwissenschaft*), thanks to "the crowd" that misperceived their field's importance and misused its key terms in increasingly broadened, literalized ways. Through repetition, revision, and the "dull regimental routine" of normal science, terms like "organic" and "linguistic organism" became more and literal, losing what Nietzsche would call their "sensuous force" as metaphors. Perhaps Nietzsche had comparative philology on his mind when he wrote a year or so later about people's inability to deal with reality without making use of a "movable host of metaphors, metonymies, and anthropomorphisms" (1979[1873]:77).

Certainly core terms of the new science of language were transformed in sense and significance when comparative philologists spoke as public intellectuals about questions of national culture, politics, and history, and as they created the first academic discipline which had "evolution as its very core" (Hobsbawm 1964:337). So it is important here to trace the development of philological notions of "evolution," and show how this science produced what Stephen Alter calls a "master metaphor" of a range of disciplines: "comparative mythology, comparative jurisprudence . . . [and] Indo-European studies in general" (Alter 1999:109), and eventually Darwinian natural history. In this way, finally, comparative philology provided evolutionary support for ideologies of European empire.

This chapter is centered on two ways that philological images of language were influential beyond the academy. The first is the broadly organic view of history which helped to explain Europe's superiority in a colonial present, naturalize its ongoing civilizational advancement, and frame linguistic difference as human inequality in a colonial world. The second centers on philology as a very German science which made the past into a resource for nationalist ideologies in an industrializing Europe, nowhere more importantly than in Germans' confrontations with a political and cultural crisis of identity quite close to home.

By focusing on the progressive loss of these organic metaphors' "sensuous force," I frame a sketch which must be somewhat repetitious, bypassing abstruse details which distinguished and marked the field's progress. It may seem specious to focus more on broad pronouncements than painstaking empirical work, especially when connections between the two are not always clear. The tenuousness of some of these broad claims based on narrow descriptions was not lost on some of these German philologists' clear-eyed contemporaries, including the German-trained American William Dwight Whitney. In his 1873 review of an essay on language origins by one German philologist, he commented acidly on the tendency of Germans to present "a minimum of valuable truth wrapped up in a maximum of sounding phraseology" (Whitney 1873:292). But what seems otherwise to be a mixing of empirical wheat and rhetorical chaff is important here for understanding how philologists used linguistic diversity to confirm the place of Germany in the world, and the superiority of what is now called "The West" over "The Rest". In this way their work helped provide a linguistic image of what Nietzsche called the "sum of human relations," metaphors of evolution which became "intensified, transferred, and embellished" in broader projects of colonialism on one hand, and nationalism on the other.[1]

The Brothers Schlegel

Before 1806, Liah Greenfeld (1992:278) has argued, no idea of nationalism existed among German speakers. But by 1815 it had already come of age among members of a "peculiar class of educated commoners, professional intellectuals" who were afflicted by an "oppressive sense of status-inconsistency" after the demise of the Holy Roman Empire. Greenfield identifies 1806 as a formative year in this development because it was then that Napoleon humiliated an overconfident Prussian army at Jena, forced the king to cede almost half his realm to the French, and threw what were then still called "the Germanies" into crisis.

Johann Herder, a member of Greenfeld's group of proto-nationalists, had already been engaged with this very crisis of identity when he wrote his speculative account of language origins discussed in chapter 3. His celebration of local, expressive authenticity inspired others who were likewise grappling with the political and cultural crisis brought on by Prussia's defeat, including the brothers Friedrich and August von Schlegel. They were to broaden Herder's ideas in their own work of comparison between languages and literatures.

Friedrich, born in 1772, might be called a visionary rather than a founder of philology thanks to his 1808 book *The language and wisdom of the Indians*. This helped promote the flow of new knowledge about India to German via Paris, intellectual crossroads of Europe, where Friedrich studied Sanskrit with one Alexander Hamilton, a retired army officer in the East India Company who later became Britain's first Sanskrit professor.

Friedrich von Schlegel sought to develop a systematic understanding of historical relations between Europe and Asia by paying more attention to the grammatical elements of languages than the lexical material which William Jones made the object of his etymological speculations. Schlegel recognized grammar to be a more coherent domain for study, its elements being far fewer than indefinitely large vocabularies, and recurring more frequently as "obligatory" components of language use. Like his brother August and his successors, he approached these elements with a founding typological distinction between languages whose grammars counted as "organic" or "mechanical." This distinction was supported, in his view, in two different ways: by differences in the structures of languages, and the ways they changed over time.

For Friedrich, "organic" languages – Sanskrit, Persian, and those of Europe – shared a common grammatical technique he called "Flexion": their words were obligatorily comprised of roots and additional elements marking number, tense, gender, etc. On the other hand "mechanical" languages – Chinese, Coptic, Basque, Amerindian languages, and Arabic (Koerner 1990:250) – had more primitive grammatical elements, called "Affixa" by Friedrich, which attached more loosely to word roots.

The superiority of organic languages endowed with "flexion," Friedrich argued, is evident in their suitability for comparative and historical analysis. They are not passive in the face of external forces like mechanical languages, which possess no internal coherence or capacity to maintain their continuity over time. Because grammars of mechanical languages have an accidental character and artificial complexity, he argued, it is "nearly impossible to trace them to a common ancestor" (Koerner 1990:250). Because organic languages actively engage with historical forces, reshaping themselves rather than passively suffering change, they are more than mere objects of historical forces, and so can be studied in and with history. In this way Friedrich gave Herder's broad organismic vision of language empirical purchase for questions about historical relatedness of languages, proposing that grammatical categories offered a means for comparing languages "in a similar way as comparative anatomy has illuminated the higher natural history" (Schlegel 1808, quoted in Koerner 1990:243, my translation).

August von Schlegel, Friedrich's brother, extended and particularized the organic image further in his studies of literary history, which did not yet count as a field distinct from that of grammar. In 1818 he gave a series of lectures on the diversity and development of genres of verbal art using a distinction much like his brother's to distinguish two kinds of literary form. A text has mechanical form "when, through external force, it is imparted to any material as an accidental addition without reference to its quality. . . . Organical form . . . is innate; it unfolds itself from within, and acquires its determination contemporaneously with the perfect development of the germ" (Schlegel 1965[1818]:340).

This "lesson of history" offered a broader moral, which August drew by echoing Herder. These facts of literature demonstrated how a true poetic spirit develops "according to laws derivable from its own essence" (Schegel 1965[1818]:340), working in accord with (its own) nature rather than laboring under "the authority of the ancients" (1846:339). These remarks allowed August to introduce comments on a more immediate problem into his discussion of Provençale literature: the Francophile Prussian nobility which, like Herder, he criticized for turning away, unnaturally, from its own language, culture, and identity. August concluded his lectures with a veiled reference to these "persons of higher ranks, [who] by their predilection for foreign manners . . . have long alienated themselves from the body of the people" (Schegel 1965[1818]:529).

By embedding the study of grammar and literature in history, the Schlegel brothers helped invest "language" with larger political and cultural meanings. At the same time they lent empirical weight to Herder's speculative ideas about language origin and change, while proclaiming that Germans must recognize their language and literature's organic vitality if they were not to risk what August called "disappearing altogether from the list of independent nations" (Schegel 1965[1818]:529).[2]

Wilhelm von Humboldt

The year after his lectures on Provençale literature, August von Schegel accepted the chair of Sanskrit at the University of Bonn, where he further elaborated his brother's typological approach to grammar. He owed this appointment, and much intellectual inspiration, to a friend and fellow scholar: Wilhelm von Humboldt, whose studies of Kawi language I discussed briefly in chapter 3. Later in the 19th century, von Humboldt came to be known as the "cofounder of the new linguistics" (Benfey 1869:279), but he had made another place for himself in Prussian history through his work as architect of an entirely new system of national education.

King Wilhelm, galvanized by his disastrous defeat at Jena, swept away the fragmented, backward-looking noble class ruling a patchwork of 1,800 tiny territories. He abolished serfdom and permitted non-nobles to own land; he removed the guild's stranglehold on crafts and professions; he instituted new forms of local self-government. Beyond all of these moves, he saw the need for a new class of governing officials, and an entirely new set of institutions to educate its members. He summoned Wilhelm von Humboldt to design them.

A wealthy noble, steeped in the study of Latin and Greek, von Humboldt had spent much of his life in close contact with intellectuals and language scholars in western Europe, not Prussia. But he answered his king's call, returning to Berlin in 1809 to help devise an educational response to his country's crisis. He did this work as a child of the Enlightenment, but also as a scholar deeply imbued with Herder's sense of language as "the outer appearance of the spirit of a people" (von Humboldt 1988[1836]:46). During his one year in service to the king he achieved at least the reputation of having designed an entirely new, language-centered system of Prussian education (Holquist n.d.:31) in which those seeking to become teachers were required to devote years of study to Latin and Greek.

Philology had a central place in von Humboldt's new universities, and his efforts to create "a German national identification with the classical past centered around ancient Greece as . . . a cultural ideal to which German education aspired" (Benes 2001:175). As German scholars and institutions became pre-eminent in the field, they were able to demonstrate historical parallels between the politics of Prussian resistance to the French in contemporary Europe, and the politics of a politically fragmented Greece which had been dominated by Rome, but was still united by a superior language and culture.

Today von Humboldt is known to linguists much less for his studies of Kawi, discussed in chapter 3, than for a grammatical typology he developed in the introduction to his voluminous body of work. That introduction, still in print – in translation with the title *On language: the diversity of human language structure and its influence on the mental development of mankind* (von Humboldt 1988[1836]) – extended the Schlegels' line of thought by distinguishing not two but four types of grammar. Languages whose words consist of single elements, like Chinese, von Humboldt counted as "isolating" languages, "with no grammatical structure" and so in his view (and August's) as essentially flawed as a means for intellectual expression (Schlegel 1965[1818]:14). Other languages, many spoken in North America, combine words to create more complex words, with grammars von Humboldt called "agglutinating." A third group of languages, represented by Basque, which von Humboldt himself had studied, have grammars he called "incorporating" or "polysynthetic" to describe the ways they fuse words into inseparable wholes which were equivalent to entire sentences.

In the fourth category von Humboldt, like August von Schlegel, placed the "first rank" of languages: those that have inflecting grammars. Words in languages like Greek, Latin, and Sanskrit (but not Javanese, as we saw in chapter 3) incorporate obligatory modifying grammatical elements which count as signs of "a living principle of development and increase." These languages alone have "fecund and abundant vegetation" (von Humboldt 1988[1836]:86).

This global comparative perspective which von Humboldt brought to bear on his reading of Kawi would, he thought, help to answer "the difficult question" of whether "languages are able or not to gradually change in nature, to pass from the first class to the second, and from the second to the third. If it were possible to respond to these questions with facts as certain evidence, a mass of problems relating to the origins of civilization would be thereby resolved" (von Humboldt 1988[1836]:85, fn.7).

Sanskrit and other inflected languages could serve as reference points, von Humboldt explained, because in them "the mental cultivation of mankind has evolved most happily in the longest sequence of advances. We can therefore regard them as a fixed point of comparison for all the rest" (von Humboldt 1988[1836]:216).

Javanese grammar "suffers ... from the Chinese lack of inflection ... [but] does not, like Chinese reject grammatical formation with scornful resignation" (von Humboldt 1988[1836]:191). So the organism of Javanese failed to move beyond its initial, "formative" period, or to achieve the kind of "elaboration" (*Ausbuildung*) which would lift it above the rank of derivative languages and civilization.

These joined questions about grammar and history were a constant element of philological efforts to make the past speak to the present, and to single out one group of languages and peoples from all others. Philological images of civilizational history, running from Greece to Germany, seized the imagination of some Germans so powerfully during this time that they ventured into the Caucasus mountains in search of "their" people's original locale and language. By 1823 Germans were studying there under sponsorship from the Russian czar, who had strategic interests of his own in the area. They contributed to the conjectural history of Indo-Germanic peoples who were understood to have migrated from the Caucasus as one of the 13 "main tribes" (*Stammvolker*) who survived the biblical flood (Benes 2001, 2004). It was this image of the past, regularized and elaborated by the philologists I discuss below, which was popularized late in the 19th century by the German philologist Max Müller as the story of the Aryans, and later was appropriated by the Nazis in the 20th century. I discuss this image of the past later as a template for the stories linguists devised about other peoples as colonial subjects, and for purposes of colonial regimes.

Franz Bopp

Von Humboldt and the Schlegel brothers' sweeping vision now seems unscientific because of the ways it blurs lines between spheres of study: speech and text, grammar and history, language and culture. Science involves procedures and questions which produce a tighter empirical focus, and insulates data from extraneous considerations. In this respect, another breakthrough to the science of language can be found in the work of Franz Bopp, von Humboldt's own tutor in Sanskrit, who published in 1816 *On the conjugation system of Sanskrit in comparison with those of Greek, Latin, Persian and German languages.*

Bopp, unlike von Humboldt, came to ancient texts not as "literary monuments" – expressions of the genius of a people, or windows on distant cultures – but as repositories of examples of usage. He found there the specific data he could abstract to develop a rigorous, comparative metric for grammatical study. He developed a more abstract notion of linguistic form, isolating part-for-whole relations between roots and grammatical elements as the core of "the true organism of a language" (quoted in Perceval 1987:7). It was this organism which, under close study, would allow for new understandings of "physical and mechanical laws" of operation, and "the origin of the forms which indicate grammatical relations."

Philology in this way became truly anatomical because texts were used "to describe the organism of a language for its own sake," as Bopp wrote in 1829 to von Humboldt (quoted in Davies 1987:89). When a language was understood to be a "natural body," its properties could be traced to the ways they "form themselves according to definite laws, develop carrying in themselves an internal life principle, and gradually die" (quoted in Davies 1987[1836]:84). New rigor allowed narrower criteria for evaluating languages through their grammatical properties, as Bopp argued, by distinguishing languages that have grammar (*Grammatik*) and so an organism (*Organismus*) from those that do not. By this measure, Chinese counted (again) as lowest among the world languages, and the Semitic languages a bit higher thanks to their disyllabic, triconsonantal roots. But both types of language were in turn inferior to others whose monosyllabic roots are capable of compounding, "acquir[ing] their organism, their grammar, almost only in this way" (quoted in Davies 1987:85). These are languages of the family now called Indo-European, which are unmatched in the "beautiful joining of these complements into a harmonic whole with the appearance of an organic body" (quoted in Davies 1987:85).

With this new analysis of form, Bopp joined grammar to history in another way: organic languages are dynamic, autonomous, and change in accord with their internal developmental logics. Other languages' "variously disfigured and mutilated forms" are evidence of their lack of such principles of internal development, and their passivity in the face of historical forces which change them.

Jakob Grimm

At the same time Bopp was developing his rigorous approach to linguistic diversity, Jakob Grimm was publishing discoveries about a narrower range of languages in a shallower, predominantly Germanic period of history. But this work brought him major stature as a philologist and public intellectual. Born in 1785 in French-occupied Prussia, into marginally middle-class conditions, Jakob made his way in the world with his younger brother as a scholar whose different projects served a single end: recapturing and resuscitating the true heritage of German-speaking peoples. The brothers Grimm heard Herder's call for cultural renewal very clearly, as can be seen in the title of a journal they established in their youth: *Old German forests (Altdeutsche Walder)*, devoted to "customs, laws, and norms that bound German people to each other" (Seitz 1984:48, quoted in Zipes 1988:45). This title echoes that which Herder chose for four volumes of his own early nationalist writings, *Critical forests* (1769).

The Grimms undertook a massive dictionary project, now far less famous than their collection of folk stories which remained incomplete at their deaths. But in the course of his work on that project, Jakob came to recognize that there were systematic patterns of sound difference between words of modern German, older German, and a range of related languages. From these patterns he inferred that they were all linked to each other by an extended historical process of sound shift (*Lautverschiebung*). In his compendious grammar of German he set these patterns out as the basis of what came to be known as Grimm's law – "If non-specialists know anything about historical linguistics, it is Grimm's law. The history of views on the consonant shift is virtually a history of linguistic theory until 1875" (Lehmann 1967:46).

Grimm demonstrated a general, systematic correspondence between subsets of the consonants found in western European languages, as they appeared in certain positions in cognate words. He noticed for instance that words in Gothic texts which were spelled with an *f* had Greek counterparts spelled with the equivalent of *p*, while their Old High German counterparts were words spelled with *b*. These patterns were *general* because they extended across a wide range of words, allowing Grimm to demonstrate part-for-whole relations between three trios of sounds: one pronounced with the lips and/or teeth ($p/b/f$), a second with the tongue and teeth ($t/d/th$), and a third in the back of the tongue and mouth ($k/g/ch$). These patterns were *systematic* because the only way to account for these correspondences was to recognize that each was nested in a larger whole, each trio linked to the others: $p/t/k$ underwent similar changes, over and against $b/d/g$ and $f/th/ch$.[3]

This was a discovery about language which brought "deep" history close to home, and so had immediate purchase on the literate German-speaking public. Grimm had shown how everyday speech bound them organically, through speech, to their ancestors in a kind of intimate but unconscious project, working itself through between generations and across centuries. Right under their noses, the German language's historical unity was being created and recreated by speakers every day.

Grimm's life work drew inspiration from Herder's philosophy, but he avoided pronouncing on the question of language origins until very late in his career. In 1851, he finally brought comparative philology, the new science of language, to bear on that old problem. After King Friedrich Wilhelm II invited him to join and address the Royal Academy of Sciences in Berlin – his progressive nationalist politics had cost him a job at the University of Gottingen – Grimm took up the problem of language origins by demonstrating (again) how organic languages are bound up with the broader developmental dynamics of human history. He presented his law of sound change as empirical evidence that "perfected inflections for grammar" arise from processes of development, and as part of the joined ascent of language and humanity. This path led for Grimm, as for Bopp, from the polysyllabic words of an "artless," "sensory," "naïve," "garrulous period of use" to monosyllabic words which were products of grammatical simplification and superior instruments of "reason" (Grimm 1984[1851]:20). Grimm in this way located himself, his audience, and their society in the civilizational dynamic I sketched in chapter 3: the work of uncovering these developmental laws demonstrated the capacities of reason they enabled. Grimm showed how, as inheritors and witnesses to this development, modern Europeans were becoming ever freer from the limitations of linguistic form.

Through these developments the field of comparative philology came into its own as the first science of language as scholars reasoned against the grain of history to excavate original, pure, grammatical forms (Kiparsky 1974:333). In 1827 Bopp could already summarize the common substance of the philological science in a review of Jakob Grimm's (1822) grammar of German. Science had demonstrated, he asserted, that languages are

> organic bodies of nature, forming according to certain laws, develop-
> ing through an inherent life principle, dying gradually as, not under-
> standing themselves anymore, they cast off their once meaningful,
> now superficial mass of parts or forms, or mutilate them or abuse
> them for purposes for which they were not originally suited. (Bopp
> 1827:251 quoted in Schlapp 2004:377)

Schleicher's Evolutionary Tree

One last step in the literalization of organic metaphors is important here as a kind of quantum leap made by August Schleicher (1821–68). He had trained in text-centered classical philology, but after shifting to grammar-centered comparative philology he gained a considerable reputation with new strategies for organizing the enormous masses of data assembled by others. His first major publication in 1848 augmented Bopp's work with new evidence about the history of Indo-European words and grammatical units, building on the distinction between isolating, agglutinating, and inflecting languages set out above. Schleicher used comparative procedures like those sketched in chapter 3 to reconstruct languages which are now extinct (like absent "ancestor" texts) but whose properties can be deduced from those of their "descendants."

Schleicher in this way developed an account of what a linguist of the next generation (discussed in chapter 6) called "that lofty structure, the Arian 'ursprache'" (Jespersen 1894:4). Although Schleicher was not the first philologist to use the idiom of kinship to describe relations between languages – an English student of sound change had already done so (Alter 1999:10) – he gave that metaphor weight and geohistorical scope with the image of the Indo-European tree (a version of which is shown in Figure 3.2).

Schleicher was to have a broader role in intellectual history, though, when a zoologist who knew of his fondness for horticulture and botany gave him a German translation of Darwin's *Origin of species*. After reading it Schleicher wrote an open letter to his young friend, Ernst Haeckel, to assert that comparative philology not only corroborated Darwin's argument, but anticipated it. Philologists, he asserted, had already laid down the very laws Darwin sought to prove: "[t]he rules now, which Darwin lays down with regard to the species of animals and plants, are equally applicable to the organisms of languages." So, he agrees, "species stand to genus as daughters of one stock" (Schleicher 1983[1863]:33).

Schleicher in this way saw that comparative philologists had without knowing it discovered and developed "methods largely the same as that of the other natural sciences." It turned out that languages really were organisms subject to laws of evolution: some "[s]pecies and genera of speech disappear, and . . . others extend themselves at the expense of the dead. . . . Not a word of Darwin's need be changed here if we wish to apply this reasoning to languages" (Schleicher 1983[1863]:62–64).

This kind of evolutionism has rightly and long been in disrepute among linguists, who now all share William Dwight Whitney's skepticism about such pronouncements. But Schleicher's reputation was such that his letter became valuable rhetorical ammunition in England, where Darwin's supporters were seeking to convince a wider audience (and so also seeking the upper hand in debates with another well-known philologist, Max Müller, touched on below).

The fundamental flaws in this analogy, which I noted in chapter 3, did not rob it of its rhetorical and ideological power. In this way comparative philology helped to disguise the difference between two different senses and images of "evolution," which were so important for imperial ideologies that they are worth distinguishing here along lines developed by Joseph Fracchia and Robert Lewontin in their critical review of the concept.

Fracchia and Lewontin (1999) distinguish two historical dynamics which have been called "evolutionary." The one they call "transformational" is directional and articulates in ordered stages, each depending on those preceding, and so incorporating them. This broad transformational vision of change served, from the philosophy of Herder to the philology of Schleicher, to develop a teleo-logical vision of languages and so of cultures, moving from state to state in accordance with their internal "natures."

The other kind of evolution Fracchia and Lewontin call "varia-tional." This was the focus of Darwin's account of evolution, which served to explain facts of difference among members of a given species. Where comparative philology explained variation (or diver-sity) in languages as a kind of byproduct or residue of their differ-ing rates and trajectories of transformational evolution, Darwin focused on mechanisms of sexual reproduction.[4] Though he had available no strong understanding of the mechanisms of genetic transmission, Darwin recognized that reproduction was a key point of interaction between species and environments: through re-production the organism proposes, and through selection the envi-ronment disposes. Selection, then, is the name for outcomes of interaction between environments and genetically determined char-acteristics of organisms (Lewontin 2000). No directional dynamic is needed or implied in this mechanism.

Schleicher's parthogenetic image of linguistic "reproduction", as I showed in chapter 3, made it possible for his Indo-European "tree" to blur this basic conceptual difference, and so also differences between Darwinian (variational) and romanticist (transformational) views of history. Once philology had literalized metaphors of descent, language and linguistic change could be made to stand, part for whole, for communities of humans and their histories, but for natural history as well. By helping to make social Darwinism a natural fact, comparative philology demonstrated the underlying dynamics of civilizational progress, from industrialization to im-perialism, in the world at large.[5]

Recovering Origins

This quick review of comparative philology's development may seem conceptually and geographically distant from work done by linguists in zones of colonial contact which were developing so rapidly around the world at this time, just as philologists' academic agendas seem quite detached from Europe's colonial projects. But the work of linguistics in the larger colonial world was in fact guided by these philological images of the past, and required techniques that were developed and legitimized by the academy. Chapter 5 sketches this interplay in the work of colonial linguists who took their cues from philological images of the past in order to devise strategies of descriptive selection and simplification. Here it is useful to show first how philological images of the past played into the ways colonialists explained what they discovered so as to legitimize their own presence.

Well before philology came of age, the past had served as a resource for explaining linguistic complexities in the present, and for simplifying those complexities in writing. John Gilchrist, for instance, a colleague of William Jones in Bengal, deduced that the babble of speech confronting him descended from the original language of an "Indian arcadia" which had been corrupted by repeated waves of invaders, Arab and Persian, whom he likened to Norman invaders of Saxon England. He sought with his descriptions to capture a written image of that original language, and this became a model for the British language of command in northern India, called Hindustani (Cohn 1996b:37).

Colonialists of a later era used philological images of the past I have discussed here to devise broadly similar histories. They regularly had recourse to stories of war, conquest, and forced displacement as explanatory factors for linguistic diversity, preferring these to processes of emigration, trade, or cultural exchange (like that which carried South Asian writing and literature so far from home). The most famous and compelling of such images was developed by Max Müller, a German philologist whose popular writings as a professor in England helped make the story of the Aryans widely known. This involved two waves of Aryan migration/conquest out of the Caucasus, through Europe and South Asia. In the colonial era these two branches of a single family were reunited when the British came to India. Thomas Trautmann (1997) describes the meanings of this story as it played into early 19th century British debates on colonial policy, and its uses to throw still developing racial ideologies of empire into doubt.

By the beginning of the 20th century, though, it was common knowledge that the British had followed in the footsteps of an earlier wave of Aryan newcomers. The *Oxford history of India*, a standard textbook for candidates in the Indian Civil Service and higher education, described how "[f]rom the Vedic hymns it has been possible to piece together a reasonably coherent picture of the Aryan invaders on their first impact with the black, noseless (flat nosed) *dasyus* who comprised their native opponents and subjects" (Smith 1919:2).

Images of invasion – often from the north, as in South Asia – were a leitmotif of conjectural colonial histories, a series of "just so" stories to account for conditions of social and linguistic complexity which Europeans encountered and themselves intended to dominate. Highly encapsulated versions of a few such histories that were devised for regions of sub-Saharan Africa help to illustrate how this image could be transposed, and provide background for the work of colonial linguists discussed in chapter 5.

In the Senegambia region of Africa's eastern coast, for instance, French explorers and military forces encountered neighboring communities where three different languages were spoken. According to Irvine and Gal (2000), Fula was spoken over a wide area and was strongly associated with Islamic orthodoxy; Wolof was spoken predominantly in northern coastal regions by Muslims; and Sereer was the language of non-Muslims living in a more restricted area to the south. Evidence now suggests that this diversity emerged from political dynamics which contributed to Wolof's value as a language of high level political relations, and so as an advantageous second language for native speakers of Sereer.

For the French, though, this condition of asymmetric bilingualism was evidence that the Wolof had conquered the Sereer, while the Fula, for their part, were superior, lighter skinned migrants from regions in Upper Egypt to the north. They were thought to possess higher intelligence, a superior religion, and a more elaborately hierarchical society. So too it followed that their superior culture and language had a kind of trickle down influence upon the Wolof, as Wolof had on the "simple" Sereer.[6]

To the west, in central Africa, similar histories helped account for the enormous linguistic diversity Europeans encountered in the Congo. One library researcher in Europe, Gaston Van Bulck (1903–66), pieced together the linguistic map partly reproduced in Figure 4.1, a mosaic of scores of languages scattered across tiny bits of territory. The basic typological demarcation on this map – represented here by a heavy black line running roughly east and west – divides

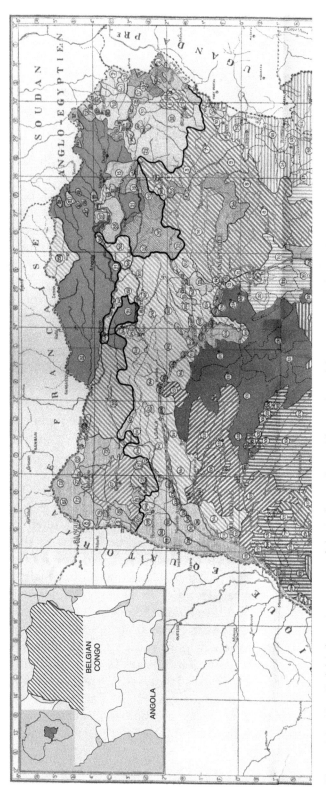

Figure 4.1 Van Bulck's linguistic map of the Belgian Congo (reproduced from Van Bulck 1948).

languages of two different families: Bantu to the south (which I discuss later) and Nilo-Saharan to the north. Van Bulck inferred from the literature then available, produced by linguists working in the region, that there were numerous tiny, moribund language "enclaves" on either side of this line. This scanty evidence sufficed for him to deduce that these were remnants of intertribal conflicts which he often described "in terms of an extended battle metaphor, reflecting his view on today's languages as winners in the survival of the fittest" (Van der Velde 1999:480).

I return to the Congo's linguistic past in chapter 5; here it is enough to see how Van Bulck's new-yet-old story of invasion and conquest could be plausible because it partook of philological images and historical narratives which had been used to conceptualize linguistic diversity elsewhere, beginning with the Indo-European languages.

Van Bulck relied heavily on work by William Bleek, a professional philologist who, quite unusually for his time, actually engaged speakers of languages he studied in their own communities. In 1862 he had published a comparative grammar of the South African languages in which he introduced the label "Bantu," still used today. (It was Bleek whose reflections on language origins elicited Whitney's sarcastic observation on the "sounding phraseology" of German writing quoted at the beginning of this chapter.) Bleek's most famous successor, Carl Meinhof, had developed this comparative enterprise into an independent academic field called Afrikanistik, breaking with older philology by claiming that he had the distinct advantage of studying languages as they were spoken. Eliciting data of speech directly from native speakers, he claimed, brought philology finally to "the life of language," and not just its "shadowy fragment[s]" in the texts studied so intensively by his Indo-Europeanist colleagues.

But from Meinhof's new science came the familiar story which Van Bulck in turn adopted and specified for the Congo. Africa was home, Meinhof argued, to three races: the Sudanic (true Negroes), Hamitic (light-skinned conquerors), and Bantu (a mixture of the two). In these names lies the kernel of Meinhof's story: Hamites entered Africa as the Aryans had India, "a superior race with the most noble physical and psychic characteristics" (quoted in Pugach 2001:41). They were closely related to Semitic speakers who had come to sub-Saharan Africa from the Middle East or Central Asia, migrating south until violent encounters with dark-skinned Negroes gave way to contact, intermarriage, and "the languages and communities we still call Bantu" (quoted in Pugach 2001:60).

The "Hamitic hypothesis" did not survive scrutiny for long, in part because it depended on the blurring of differences between race and language in empirically implausible ways. What is important here, though, are the intellectual traditions and colonial interests which gave Meinhof's account plausibility and usefulness. It framed the precolonial past to fit the colonial present, especially during Prussia's aggressive imperial African campaign in the 1870s, and survived up through Afrikaner apartheid policies in postcolonial South Africa (Pugach 2004).

As men of science and faith, Meinhof (Lutheran) and Van Bulck (Catholic) counted as scholars in the academy, not researchers in the field. Once Meinhof's "school" of African linguistics in Hamburg became a center for research with native speakers who were imported from Africa, it also became an important destination for Europeans (mostly German, many missionaries) embarking for or returning from Africa. That Meinhof was an armchair scholar in no way diminished his reputation among these visitors, including those who had grown up in Africa and had acquired native fluency in languages they came to Meinhof to study. Such was the authority of philological science that he could hold out the prospect of helping them really understand what they already knew.

From Nationalism to Colonialism and Back Again

This foreshortened sketch has focused more on dubious heuristics than substantive discoveries because I am concerned with comparative philology as a means for making linguistic diversity useful in a world of nation-states and empires. As organic metaphors became literal, images of the linguistic past took on the kind of facticity which allowed them to be transposed between places and issues: kinship and texts, language and race, grammar and history.

I have also emphasized the political and cultural contexts of these formative images as they were devised, applied, and elaborated.

Herder, the Schlegels, von Humboldt, the Grimms, and others saw their work as parts of a nationalist project, shared with other German-speaking peoples, to realize an autonomous nation. Applied locally, images of language history fitted and corroborated their shared sense of national destiny in Europe, and later, as an imperial power, the world at large. Applied globally, these same images helped to chart the long historical trajectory in which imperialism emerged as a natural continuation of the civilizational dynamic. When Europe's nation-states could be understood to have achieved historical autonomy as active, collective agents, the condition of modernity (Dirks 1990) they had come to inhabit could be extended to other places, and bestowed on other peoples. By focusing on comparative philology's evolution in Europe before turning to work of linguists abroad, I have emphasized the ways this science of language emerged within the "unitary field of analysis" (Cohn 1996a:4) of colonial history.

This sketch also suggests an important critique of Said's account of orientalism, which focused on work done by French philologists at a time when Prussia was too occupied with its own survival to embark on imperial projects abroad. The result was a split between Germans, who were the primary driving force behind philology's evolution, and the agents of imperial power who found that field ideologically useful, as Said suggests, for legitimizing projects of conquest. One symptom of this division of labor is apparent in the career of Max Müller: when the xenophobic English sought out an academic expert on India, the jewel in their imperial crown, they finally and grudgingly employed a scholar whose native country had no comparable presence in the colonialized world. (See van der Veer 2001 for further discussion.)

This transposability of linguistic images of the past to political and cultural projects in the present – for autonomy (as in Germany) and domination (as in many different colonies) – is important enough to deserve one more illustration from a situation which combined both conditions. I mentioned in chapter 3 that European missionaries had long been familiar with Tamil, a language spoken in southern India, before William Jones "discovered" Sanskrit in Bengal. The earliest descriptions of Tamil by Europeans date from 1310, well before the discovery of the New World, and by the time German Protestant missionaries arrived in the early 17th century considerable attention had been devoted to the language. Nonetheless, the vast majority of Tamil speakers recognized the religious and political superiority of members of the Brahman class who, as the story of the Aryans explained, were superior by virtue of their genealogical and cultural inheritance: the original Hindu religious tradition and its Truth language, Sanskrit.

After Jones published his findings on relations between languages of Europe and those of northern India, another British civil servant working in Madras, Francis Ellis, published his own findings on relations between languages spoken to the south.[7] These became better known in 1856 when Robert Caldwell, a Scottish missionary, published a comparative grammar of these so-called Dravidian languages, demonstrating philologically that Tamil and neighboring languages stood together as a group over and against languages spoken to the north, including Sanskrit. He went on to speculate about the origins of a Tamil Dravidian culture, suggesting that a pure Tamil language could be traced back to the time of Christ, and that Aryan Brahman colonists had only arrived, with their religion and language, much later.

By the end of the century, Tamils who had been exposed to British educational institutions and ideas assumed a new, politically motivated stance to this picture of the past. It gave them grounds for rejecting the notion that the "Aryan" cultural tradition was older than, different from, and superior to their own, and fueled a debate about the facts and meanings of Tamil and Dravidian linguistic autonomy. This debate engaged with the status of the small, dominant, Brahman fraction of Tamil society, who were distinguished as the direct inheritors of Sanskritic knowledge (Irschik 1969).

Harold Schiffman (1996) has drawn on work by Sumathi Ramaswamy (1993) to sketch this as a philological debate between "Compensatory Classicists," who argued from philological evidence that Tamil in the past had been on a par with Sanskrit, and the "Contestatory Classicists," who argued that Tamil's superiority to Sanskrit had only been obscured by invaders from the north. But both parties agreed on a central point: an originary, "pure" Tamil language could be recovered even after it had been sullied by representatives of an outside power. Images of language purity thus began to figure in longstanding contests over the proper genres of liturgical speech (Appadurai 1981; Schiffman 1996) in an ethnonational separatist movement opposed not to the power of British colonialists (at first), but other colonized ethnic groups to the north.

Even sketched so briefly, this final example helps to show that although William Dwight Whitney's complaints about "sounding phraseology" distorting "valuable [philological] truth" were entirely legitimate, they did not speak to the ideological power of the metaphors which that phraseology repeated and expanded across conceptual spheres. With a broad sense of the development of philological images of evolution, we can consider their meanings and uses in particular zones of colonial contact, where linguists undertook the formidable challenge of reducing the speech of colonial subjects to writing.

Notes to chapter 4

1 Interested readers could recast this brief review of the development of philology in terms used by Pierre Bourdieu (1993) to account for the dynamics in a wide range of literary and academic "fields," but that is beyond the scope of this chapter.
2 I must ignore here questions of class which, as Greenfeld indicates, were crucial for Herder and other romantics' self-positioning in relation to "the people" (*das Volk*). Discussion of this important issue can be found in Bauman and Briggs 2003.
3 Grimm's "discovery" was in fact anticipated by the Danish philologist Rasmus Rask, and counted as a "law" in no more than a rhetorical sense.
4 Adaptations of evolutionary theory to the study of language change and contact are far from dead; see for instance Mufwene 2001.
5 Darwin himself crossed this line, in the other direction, in *The descent of man* (1936b[1871]), to distinguish not just between animals and men, but "modern" men and "savages" of the "lower races." Nowadays sociobiologists have more sophisticated versions of transformational understandings of history as "evolution." They assume that some natural (genetically determined) properties of humans confer on them relatively broader adaptive abilities across a range of natural environments, and so have broadly directional shaping effects on cultural transmission, which turns out to be a subform of natural selection. But this idea was already at the heart of Herder's account of language

origins which I sketched in chapter 3, which began with the riddle of the human species' relatively weak senses, but strong adaptive capacities.

6 For extended, insightful discussion of a wider range of French scholarship of African languages, see Irvine 1993, 1995, and 2001.

7 For discussion of the development of Ellis' work in scholarly interchange with scholarly speakers of these languages, see Trautmann 2006.

Chapter 5

Between Pentecost
and Pidgins

*Each village has its own language; take this then to pray to our
Father!*
And the Lord will understand our poor and needy word
Dida hymn of the Harrist Church, Ivory Coast (quoted in Krabill
1995:253)

*To make him talk pidgin is to fasten him to the effigy of him, to snare
him, to imprison him, the eternal victim of an essence, of an appearance for which he is not responsible.*
Frantz Fanon, *Black skin, white masks* (1967:35)

In this chapter I discuss work of linguists who helped to make the
19th century not just an age of empire but of missions, as "the rather
idiosyncratic concern of a handful of Moravians" in 1780 became
by 1840 "almost the very raison d'être of the all the mainline
churches as understood by their more lively and enthusiastic membership" (Hastings 1994:245).[1] From the enormous body of work
about languages spoken all over the missionized world I draw here
on a few examples, mostly from sub-Saharan Africa, to discuss the
purposes, social imaginaries, and practices of literacy which shaped
their content (sometimes inaccurate), uses (sometimes conflicted),
and long-term effects (sometimes unforeseen and unintended).

The work of missionaries has attracted increasing interest among
historians, anthropologists, and literary scholars who recognize that
missionaries were agents of some of the most intimate forms of

colonial power. Reading critically in the archives has offered insights into the gentler, more pervasive micropolitics of missionary authority, and the kinds of conflictedness which enabled it. One common dilemma facing missionaries arose from their double engagement with colonial subjects as well as other colonial agents, institutions, and interests. They might believe that they were "men [*sic*] of God and ambassadors for Christ [who] have nothing to do with trade in any way whatever"(quoted in Hastings 1994:284), but they needed support of fellow citizens of Europe's colonial powers. They might have regarded the brutal use of power as means to God's real end, which they served "following at a distance, in the rear of victorious armies, to plant her stations," as a minister preached to the London Missionary Society in 1819 (quoted in Thorne 1999:38). But missionaries were obliged to accept the authority and agendas of powerful colonial institutions, particularly when their work of conversion involved educational projects which helped create hierarchies of people and language alike.

Broadly similar callings, goals, and circumstances make it easy to overlook differences between missionaries' social backgrounds which had shaping effects on their work. Some missionaries were marginal or self-marginalized in their "home" countries; others embraced the double authority of their nation and their religion. Some were highly educated; others had only limited literacy in their own languages. Some were profoundly transformed by years spent with "their" natives; others were loyal soldiers of Christ among pagans they neither understood nor trusted. Each had what can be called, using James Clifford's word for the work of anthropology, a preterrain, comprised of "all those places you have to go through and be in relation with just to get to your village or to that place of work you will call your field" (Clifford 1992:100).

Faith, status, and nationality are useful categories for considering such differences between missionaries' stances and strategies, and their more or less successful work as linguists (describing languages), teachers (of literacy), and preachers (to pagans). Reading their linguistic work with an eye to the times and places they produced it, as well the languages they described, helps to get a sense of how they developed the strategies of selection which allowed simple written images to substitute for complex worlds of speech. This way of reading also helps to recognize how that work was shaped by the institutions and ideologies which made it possible, legitimate, and useful in larger regimes of colonial power.

This chapter's two epigraphs help to emphasize religious belief as a basic grounding for all of this work, in the 19th century as in the 16th. The first is an exhortation translated from a hymn sung in the Dida language in Harrist churches on the Ivory Coast. It calls on God's children to worship in their own languages, evoking a Pentecostal sense that those words are needy not because they are primitive or uncivilized, but because they are human.[2] The second epigraph is Franz Fanon's protest against the psychopathology afflicting those who cannot avoid having a "pidgin" version of a "real" language affixed to their senses of self. Fanon's protest can be read as warning more broadly against severe dislocating effects of linguistic descriptions which might have had an aura of colonial authority, but failed to present colonial subjects with recognizable, written images of their own speech. Such a linguistic effigy of speech could be imposed by colonial regimes as a model for language, and have far-reaching effects on senses of linguistic sharedness and community under colonial regimes.

Faith and Literacy, Faith in Literacy

Differences between Protestant and Catholic strategies of conversion broadly reflected their faiths, and shaped their engagements with pagan languages. Like the friar linguists discussed in chapter 2, Catholic missionaries in the 19th century were concerned mainly to induct their converts into a global community of ritual and belief. They understood that their calling was to mediate between the Latinate body of textual Truth and new converts in "vocalized exchange between God and the priest, and between the priest and the hearer" (Peterson 2004:122). An understanding of the gist of faith sufficed, in their view, for natives to participate in the orthodoxies of Catholic religious and social practice. Catholic missionaries who regarded linguistic difference as a barrier to conversion to be overcome had little reason to invest much time in describing or learning their converts' languages. Instead they sought out languages which were widely spoken, natively or not, across groups, and which were relatively prestigious among different communities (like Nahuatl, the *lengua general* of Mexico). Some used the languages of colonial regimes to Christianize and civilize their converts, which I discuss this in chapter 6.

Protestants understood that biblical truth could only come directly to individuals through personal knowledge of that text, and so that they were called to provide translations which could produce internal conversions of mind, imagination, and soul. For them, the gift of faith went with the gift of literacy, and so the ability to "read the Word through their individual, cognitive work" (Peterson 2004:122). For native languages to become bridges to faith, then, Protestant missionaries engaged local speechways as means for "transform[ing] interior worlds" (Meyer 1999:38) through practices of literacy. From the earliest, "idiosyncratic Moravians" of the late 18th century[3] up to missionary work going on today, touched on in chapter 7, faith and literacy were constantly joined in the work of Protestant missionaries. Richard Lepsius, a philologist who lent his expertise to this global endeavor, explained that only when "the Word of God is read by the people themselves, and where a whole people are made susceptible of the spirit of Christianity by the distribution of the Bible and of Christian school-books can a rapid, a deep and lasting work be hoped for" (Lepsius 1855:6).

So it is "not surprising," as William Samarin observes, "that Protestant missionaries would have had more interest in the native languages and that Protestants would have been even more committed to learning them than Catholics" (1984:436). This meant, though, that Protestant missionaries were committed to a double paradox of translation and conversion. All missionaries relied on faith to draw lines between what in pagan lives could be preserved and what had to be banished. But to acquire the languages they needed for that work, they had to engage with the lives of those languages' speakers in their entirety, what one American missionary more recently referred to in the jargon of social science as "the totality of a social system." To refuse full engagement with a community would produce linguistic knowledge as a broken, pidgin idiom "suitable for dealings only with individuals who are peripheral in the community at large" (Smalley 1958 paraphrased by Beidelman 1982:17). To avoid learning and using the kind of broken, pidgin language Fanon criticizes, missionaries needed sustained contact with the full range of non-Christian speechways and lifeways.[4]

This was seen clearly by one of the colonial era's most distinguished linguists. Hermann Neubronner van der Tuuk was employed in the 1850s by a Dutch missionary organization (the Nederlands Zendeling Genootschap, or NZG, which I discuss below) to translate Christian texts into the Batak language, spoken by peoples of the interior of the island of Sumatra. Van der Tuuk was no devout Christian, but had no qualms about the work of christianizing Bataks who could then serve as buffers between Dutch settlements in the southern parts of Sumatra, and anticolonial Islamic peoples to the north and west.

In 1867, with the benefit of hindsight, van der Tuuk drew a moral from his work with the Batak in a letter to a friend written with a "pen dipped in bile": "[a]nyone who learns a language for the purpose of translating the Bible into it is nothing but a villain, and therefore I have more contempt for myself than for anyone else" (1962:109). Van der Tuuk acknowledged gaps of meaning between his translations and the Batak language, due to his partial knowledge of the language's uses and speakers. This ignorance was required of him by his employers, who regarded any close engagement with pagans as possibly tainting their missionaries' faith. "To learn a language well," van der Tuuk continued, "one must become familiar with its community (*volk*), and this for some nations (*natiën*) is not possible except by considering their religion. And it is exactly this which would count as a deadly sin for a society that lives by bigotry"[5] (1962:109). The bitterness of van der Tuuk's complaint against his own "nation" (the Netherlands) and employers arose from his professional frustration with his descriptive "effigy" of the Batak language. He surely knew also that less talented, observant, or committed linguists were unlikely to even recognize, let alone resolve, the dilemma he came to see as a founding condition for all their work.

The second common dilemma was more pressing for some missionaries than others: the uses and effects of their linguistic work always outran their own purposes. This problem was most acute for those who adhered to the romanticist, organic vision of the

earliest German missionaries, and distinguished categorically
between the work of christianizing pagans and civilizing primitives. They sought to provide the gift of faith without creating an
avenue of entry for secular institutions or ideas. This vision of language, locale, and identity was encapsulated in the ideal of a national
Church (*Volkskirche*) which was to be "planted in the soil of heathen
nations [so] that [they] become . . . naturalized there as a domestic
growth" (Meyer 1999:34). One influential Swiss missiologist
appealed to this ideal of a truly native Christianity in the 1870s with
a warning to missionaries against any sense of "cultural superiority
and . . . national egoism" (Warneck 1901:104). Their lack of flexibil-
ity would lead to a "lack of pedagogic skill in dealing with those
who are the objects of missions," and so to the "birth of a feeling of
inferiority" among them.

This split vision, which sought to avoid "confounding . . . Chris-
tianisation with Europeanisation or Americanisation," reflects a
tension which ran throughout the work of missionaries under colonial regimes, including the linguistic descriptions they devised and
practices of literacy they taught. Beyond the ideological difficulties
involved in maintaining this distinction, missionaries faced practical difficulties wherever they did not exercise exclusive oversight
over every aspect of their converts' lives, but instead were located
with those converts in broader networks of colonial power and
hierarchies. Then their linguistic descriptive work served not just
to teach literacy, but to incorporate those they converted as subjects
of colonial regimes.

A useful, somewhat extreme, example of this merging of the
work of faith/literacy and projects of power can be drawn from
New Zealand's early colonial history, where missionaries provided
a pretext and means for incorporating their new flocks into an
emerging British empire. Missionaries established a school there in
1815 to begin teaching an improvised system of Maori writing
which was later improved on by one of the missionaries who
returned to England with two Maori chiefs in 1820. They consulted
with a Cambridge professor of Arabic to devise a grammar and
vocabulary of "the language of New Zealand" which they took back
to the islands as the template for locally printed materials. By 1830,
English observers happily reported, written materials had spread
widely enough that Maoris were acquiring literacy "with a degree

of decorum and regularity which would have reflected credit on a school of the same kind in England" (quoted in McKenzie 1985:14).

What now seems a delusional analogy between English and Maori societies counts as evidence of Protestant doxa's shaping power on those who perceived the Maori as untainted innocents, and candidates for salvation ready to "naturally" take over faith and practices of literacy together. Another observer predicted three years later that "[t]he day is not far distant, when the people generally will be able to read for themselves, in their own tongue, the wonderful works of God" (quoted in McKenzie 1985:18). This shows how easy it was for outsiders to find what they "wanted to find, [and] report what [they] knew their London [missionary] committee wished to hear" (McKenzie 1985:16). (This "committee" was the London Missionary Society, discussed below.)

This same interested, partial vision made possible the now infamous ritual which ushered the Maori into the colonial era in 1840: the signing of the Treaty of Waitangi. The soon-to-be governor of New Zealand assembled Maori chiefs at Waitangi to sign a document which officially and legally ceded their authority to the British. First proclaimed aloud in English, and then in a Maori translation, it was dubious in the first place because it incorporated a large number of words (actually, just the sounds of those words) from English into Maori. When these unintelligible sounds had been uttered in the presence of ears which could not grasp their meaning, or the import of the act of reading itself, the gathered chiefs made their marks at the bottom of the paper, contributing to a ritual of literacy whose context and effects they could not understand.

As long as the British could regard these chiefs as "literate," in some sense of the word, their acts could be regarded as binding, even if the cultural gap glossed over in this way was glaring enough to lead one witness – the printer of Maori literacy materials – to ask the new governor if the chiefs understood what they were signing. The governor responded that they should trust in the advice of "their" missionaries, and expressed the hope that no "reaction" would follow should they come to apprehend later what they did not understand at the moment. This bland observation reflected a thin sense of legitimacy, based on an implausible refusal of linguistic difference, not unlike that which legitimized readings of the

Requerimiento by the Conquistadores in the New World (discussed in chapter 2). There is no record, though, of any witness at Waitangi who was left not knowing whether to laugh or cry, like Bartolomeo de las Casas in Mexico.

The treaty of Waitangi provides a clear example of the ways literacy allowed regimes of power to be bound up with the work of faith. But missionaries elsewhere found themselves to be accomplices of other kinds of power, as happened to linguists working on another island at about the same time: Madagascar.

The Scholarizing Project

The vagaries of politics in Europe, along with Madagascar's location off the east coast of Africa, led to a situation in which missionaries worked more than 60 years before Madagascar was formally colonized by France in 1895, very late in the imperial game. In his insightful description of linguistic work by missionaries there, Louis Raison-Jourde traces far-reaching effects of the practices of literacy missionaries used to describe the Imerina language, and so christianize and "scholarize" its speakers.

Madagascar had for centuries been a meeting point for traders between Asia and Africa, and was divided into small kingdoms stratified into classes of nobles, commoners, and slaves. By 1642, the French had managed to establish only small footholds on the coast, and not until a century and a half later were the British finally able to gain an alliance with the king of the inland realm, Radama I (ruled 1810–28), through the time-honored technique of entering a local struggle for power, and tipping the balance in favor of their future ally.

The British helped Radama expand his domain to the entire island, and induced him to end the lucrative slave trade, at least officially. The king also allowed missionaries from the London Missionary Society to join their French counterparts in opening schools in different parts of Madagascar. These missionaries, working under Radama's close supervision, were of different faiths (Protestant and Catholic), nationalities (British and French), and ethnicities (Welsh and English), all factors which exacerbated their "natural" competition for spheres of influence.

So arose one instance of a common problem for colonial linguists: missionaries of different backgrounds working in different locales produced different literacies for similar speech and, by teaching those literacies, produced different senses of linguistic identity. On Madagascar, different descriptions of Imerina, also known as Malgache, created such a situation which Radama took into his own hands. In 1823 he convened a meeting of pupils whom missionaries had taught literacy and Christianity in their different schools. As one pupil told it,

> [t]he king told us: "Write the name Rakoto," so we twelve wrote in different ways: some wrote Roccotoo or Racwootoo, or Raquootwoo, Then Radama said: "unite your two groups, unify your ways of writing so that Malgache [i.e., Imerina] writing conforms to our language. If your ways of writing are not identical, it is as if my realm isn't just mine but that of many masters." (Quoted in Raison-Jourde 1977:644, my translation)

Though illiterate, Radama was not insensitive to the political and symbolic import of a plurality of written images of Imerina: a language divided in this way would be in the hands of the "many masters" of literacies which they were teaching away from his own center of power. So he moved unilaterally to create a proprietary relation with the language by requiring that a single literacy be propagated uniformly across his territory and among his subjects.

Radama's successor, Ranavalona, helped British missionaries carry out a dictionary project not unlike that being undertaken at the same time in Germany by the Grimm brothers, discussed in chapter 4. The missionaries were dealing with two languages, not one, but also had an advantage over the Grimms: hundreds of literate native speakers worked as assistants under them on the king's orders, fostering a "scientific project, in the best tradition of the English academies or German university of the 18th and 19th centuries ... [but] taken up by the Merina state with a national significance" (Raison-Jourde 1977:645, my translation).

The writing of this dictionary involved practices of literacy which required a particular kind of "meaning" to create word-to-word relations between the elements of English and Imerina. Isolating and juxtaposing elements of alien and familiar languages in written lists required that there exist a kind of lowest common denominator of meaning. Only by assuming that a unitary "semantic field" underlay both languages could missionaries bridge enormous gaps between social imaginaries.

Like Radama before him, King Ranavalona had a political interest in this project: it promoted unity among members of the new class of literate speakers being produced by missionary schools. The dictionary contributed to the same authoritative, literate image of "the" Imerina language his predecessor had sought to create as a representation of centralized political power (Raison-Jourde 1977:645). Literate subjects could serve royal power but also threaten it, a possibility which fueled the king's suspicions of the missionaries' ulterior motives. He forced the missionaries to stop that work in 1835, even though they were allowed to continue their dictionary project.

In 1895 the French assumed control over a vastly changed Merina society dominated by scholarized, christianized elites. As in New Zealand, but more slowly, missionary linguists' work of education and faith helped to make their converts subjects of an "outside" colonial power. But in both places, as all over the colonial world of the 19th century, this work was done not just by individuals, but by institutions in the "home countries" of Europe which supported them. Most obviously, missionaries relied on the infrastructures which produced texts in the languages they described and translated for new Christians to read. Secondly, missionaries unversed in the difficulties of linguistic analysis needed broadly intellectual support for their work of reducing speech to writing. Some comparative philologists in Europe brought their science to bear on this challenge for the work of faith, trying to help missionaries avoid orthographic confusions of tongues, and enlisting them in a metropolitan project of global civilization and knowledge.

From Letters to Orthography

Though the Africanist Carl Meinhof was one of the first professional linguists in Europe to study the actualities of exotic speech, text-centered philologists were always interested in the work of reducing speech to writing. At the same time "Oriental" Jones was studying Sanskrit texts, for instance, he was also reading work by his fellow colonialist William Halhed on the "Hindoo" language of Bengal and Upper India. Halhed, like Jones and Gilchrist, inferred from Sanskrit elements he found in Hindu speech that it was a decadent version of an older, literate language. He understood also that his job was to "cultivate" the language, as Bernard Cohn puts it, by recovering authentic forms of the original language from "fallen, broken, or corrupt" speech. In the same volume of *Asiatic Researches* which presented his famous address about Sanskrit's deep linguistic past, Jones discussed Halhed's grammar in an article entitled "On the orthography of Asiatic words in Roman letters" (Jones 1788).

Jones identified two basic challenges faced by Europeans and commended Halhed for overcoming the first: defectively applying "the same letter to several different sounds, and . . . different letters to the same sound" (Jones 1788:7).[6] Jones acknowledged the imperfection of European alphabets in this respect, and their inferiority to those of scholars who created invariant, one-to-one correspondences. The second challenge, beyond the power of any individual to solve, arose from inconsistencies between different conventions established by different authors. Jones bemoaned liberties taken by writers who each devised "a method of notation peculiar to himself, but none has yet appeared in the form of a complete system, so that each original sound may be rendered invariably by one appropriate symbol, conformably to the natural order of articulation, and with a due regard to the primitive power of the Roman alphabet" (Jones 1788:1–2).

Taming the "primitive power of the Roman alphabet" was more than a matter of aligning its symbols with sounds of speech produced phonetically or, as Jones put it, a "natural order of articulation." The physiology of sound production had become an object of scientific study in Europe but, as Jones demonstrated in this article, the creating of a uniform scientific orthography required institutional coordination between all linguists studying all languages.

As the case of Imerina shows, no such uniformity had been achieved 50 years later even on one relatively small island. But over this same period of time, eminent figures in the science of comparative philology were taking up the challenge Jones had identified. Richard Lepsius, whom I quoted above on the needs of missionary linguists, was a faithful Lutheran (like Carl Meinhof) whose fame came from discoveries in Egypt and Nubia during an 1842 expedition sponsored by Fredrick William the Fourth of Prussia. Surveying the burgeoning body of linguistic descriptive work by missionaries around the colonial world, he recognized, as had Jones, that

> a diversity of signs for one and [the] same sound in different languages . . . [is a problem which] has become so great that the translator of Oriental works, the Tourist, the Geographer and Chartographer, the Naturalist, the Ethnographer, the Historian . . . and above all others the Linguist, who studies and compares languages, find themselves entangled in an intolerable confusion of orthographic systems and signs, from which each individual finds it impossible to extricate himself. (Lepsius 1855:3)

Lepsius took on the task of overcoming this Babel-like "confusion" by publishing what he envisioned as *a standard alphabet for reducing unwritten languages and foreign graphic systems to a uniform orthography in European letters.*

Phrases like "graphic system" and "orthography" reflect Lepsius' concern to identify empirical "imperfections" in received European practices of literacy, none of which "could claim in its present state to be used as a standard system." Lepsius promoted his own orthography as being grounded not just in modern science, but ancient wisdom which that science had uncovered. His discussion of what Jones called the "natural order of articulation" drew on knowledge in Sanskritic texts which his colleagues had discovered, "physiological and linguistic views more accurate than those of any other people:"

> [t]hese grammarians [of ancient Sanskrit] penetrated so deeply into the relations of sounds in their own language . . . that no language and no alphabet are better suited to serve . . . as a starting point for the construction of a universal linguistic alphabet than that of ancient India. (Lepsius 1855:15)

In this way Lepsius brought comparative philology full circle: advances in his own modern science were validated in the ancient texts which were now that science's object of interest and source of guidance.

Lepsius also recognized that for his orthography to be not just valid but widely used, it was a matter of practical importance that it be accepted by those who would oversee its use. This was a transnational collection of missionary groups – German, French, American, English, and Swiss – whose endorsements he sought and gained, and whose names are listed on the first pages of his orthography's first edition. Thanks to these endorsements, too, Lepsius' alphabet became better known than another devised by Max Müller about the same time, even if Müller had a higher popular profile for reasons noted in chapter 4.

Müller's "missionary alphabet" was also designed to overcome the "defects peculiar to each" of Europe's national literacies, recognizing that "it would be wrong to smuggle any one of these imperfect systems into those languages ... which have not yet been reduced to alphabetical writing" (Müller 1854a:xviii). Müller seems to have devoted less time to presenting his alphabet to missionary organizations than Lepsius, perhaps because he was also trying to attract the attention of Britain's diplomatic and military elite. This is evident in another work presenting this orthography, published the same year under the portentous title *Suggestions for the assistance of officers in learning the languages of the seat of war in the East* (i.e., the Crimea). In this work's introduction he noted the obstacle posed to Britain's imperial power by the fact that "[a] man-of-war is built in less time than an Oriental scholar can be launched ready to converse with natives, and capable of producing supplies, gathering information, translating proclamations, writing circulars ... and, finally, of wording the conditions of a treaty of peace" (Müller 1854b:ix).

Language, Territory, and Identity

The idea of a single, coordinated system for writing all the world's languages can be taken as a kind of secular counterpart to the vision of global Christianity that missionaries shared with each other, and offered their converts. Viewed from a distance, as toilers in the vineyards of the Lord, differences between them can be discounted, at least when considering their work as linguists. But the work of missionaries in Madagascar demonstrates that in fact they cooperated and competed with each other according to nationality, social status, and faith. Whether or not they served the same God, they were members of different denominations, citizens of different nations, occupants of different social niches, products of different educational systems. These factors all shaped their social imaginaries, their practices of literacy, and so their work of spiritual and linguistic conversion.

Virtually all missionaries abroad required material support from organizations "back home." The London Missionary Society (LMS), for instance, had dispatched missionaries to New Zealand and Madagascar, among many other places. It was founded in 1795 with financial support largely from the nonaristocratic middle class emerging in England's industrializing, urbanizing centers. Although it became the most liberal missionary group in Britain over the first part of the 19th century, it was firmly in the hands, Susan Thorne (1999) notes, of an educated middle class whose assumed superiority was duly recognized by the largely lower status missionaries they sent abroad. Similarly, the Dutch Missionary Society (NZG), which supported van der Tuuk's study of Batak in Sumatra, was "securely in the hands of a social and cultural elite which was supported by an emerging bourgeoisie" (van Rooden 1996:81). This was an organization van der Tuuk himself acidly described as depending on speculation on the pockets of "pious cheese-buyers . . . " "a pack of saints who did not care a straw for study" (van der Tuuk 1962:109).

Such organizations were founded and run by socially and religiously conservative men, even if economic and social resources came to them thanks to their new places in rapidly industrializing societies. Brigit Meyer (1999) points out that founders of Bremen's Norddeutsche Missiongesellschaft, for instance, earned profits in a new economy, but were profoundly distrustful of empirical-rational thought. They, like the heads of other such organizations, chose as their missionaries people less fortunate if no less devout than themselves: pious, rudimentarily educated, not far removed from the farm, local market, or craftshop.

The same groups which were sending missionaries abroad were doing similar work at home among those who were bearing the brunt of Europe's urbanizing, industrializing dynamics. Evangelizing and educating efforts were putting literacy and faith on offer to the new urban poor, creating another project to integrate (and subordinate) those who were otherwise marginal in the global advance of Christian civilization. Just as evangelists were working to spread literacy in countries like England, so too the expanding state-sponsored education system of France was engineering the transformation of peasants into literate citizens. In Europe as abroad, literacy was being propagated as the touchstone for new identities, standing "at the entrance of the modern world as dragons guard the gateway of a temple" (Weber 1976:452).

Whether or not they knew and used Lepsius' orthography, many missionaries embarked with neither broad education nor specific training in the work of linguistic description. They were obliged to do the work of writing and translating exotic languages by relying heavily on their own "common sense" ideas about languages generally, and practices of literacy in particular. I can sketch these by considering the ways they dealt with problems like those encountered by the friar linguists discussed in chapter 2: devising the strategies of selection to reduce complex differences in speech – between dialects of different groups, and styles used in different contexts – to simple alphabetic images.

National Languages, Communities, and Territories

Missionaries' practices of literacy and social imaginaries can be thought of as grounded in their broadest, common condition as literate citizens of 19th century nation-states. This makes it helpful to review briefly Benedict Anderson's (1991) influential, language-centered historical account of the emergence of nationally imagined communities. Nationally imagined communities became possible in Europe, Anderson argues, after print technology made it economically feasible to produce large numbers of texts for large numbers of potential readers. As early capitalists, printers sold texts, like other commodities, by maximizing their markets. They needed print-literate images of what people could recognize as "their own" speech, despite the ways it differed from place to place, or class to class. In this way print literacy became infrastructural for a sense of linguistic sharedness, both an aspect of national identities and an instrument of state institutions.

Anderson's language-centered account of nationalism draws on political and cultural changes I discussed in chapters 3 and 4 as part of comparative philology's rapid development over the 19th century. Philological images of deep human history made it possible for unitary national languages to be understood as both transhistorical and everyday realities, binding the present to the past, and the personal to the collective. Thanks to Herder and those who followed him, languages counted as evidence of how individuals were bound to society, as were their biographies to history; language became immediate evidence for the claims of groups on individuals: "my" language is already there for me before I am born, and for my descendants after I die.

Most important here are the European "cultures of standardization," to use Michael Silverstein's (1996) phrase for largely unspoken but powerful understandings of national languages as unified, coherent, and "pure." These cultures, grounded in literate images, authoritative institutions, and normative ideals, allow features of nonstandard speech to be regarded not just as differences of usage but marks of personal deficiency, often slotted into categories of race, class, gender, region, and others. Thanks to cultures of standardization, "accent" and "dialect" count as names for attributes of speech and speakers who are relatively marginal or inferior in broader social hierarchies.

Cultures of standardization thus substitute the "standard" part for diverse varieties, creating relations of "internal translation" between them. In this way a seemingly unitary national language can be thought of, as Etienne Balibar (1991:351) points out, as being not just a natural attribute of its speakers, but the territory they occupy. Like Anderson and others, Balibar links the integrity of modern nation-states to a shared sense (if not the reality) of social and linguistic homogeneity within a demarcated expanse of territory. In this way cultures of standardization, and the images of a "pure" language they support, enable a broader sense of the sharedness of ways of speaking and places of speakers.

Missionaries, as literate citizens of modern nation-states, partook of such social imaginaries and cultures of standardization, which made literacy much more than a resource for devising scientific orthographies. It was easy for them to understand that languages counted as natural bonds between speakers and territories, and to read complexities of speech as secondary to the underlying reality of a unitary language. If languages' forms and attributes were disguised by blooming, buzzing confusions of speech, they could nonetheless be re-created in written and print-literate images. Cultures of standardization could shape the work of description by allowing language-centered ideas about society and identity to be projected onto potential converts; in this way practices of print literacy could transform communities to fit European understandings of how languages were located on the territories given to missionaries as their "fields of operation."

Here I sketch just two of the many such projects of missionaries around the colonial world who partly described and partly created languages and communities of converts. They were carried out in neighboring parts of subequatorial Africa, beginning in the late 19th century, and each is useful here as a kind of political and linguistic mirror-image of the other. One was done in southern Rhodesia (now Zimbabwe) where missionaries of different faiths and nationalities transformed an area of relative linguistic homogeneity into a region where speakers of distinct languages had distinct colonial identities. In the Transvaal, to the southeast, missionaries who encountered an area of massive linguistic diversity worked, with faith and philological images of the past, to impose an image of linguistic unity, and with it new religious and cultural identities.

Many from one: dialect and language in Shonaland

Zimbabwe is linguistically homogeneous in comparison with many regions and nations of Africa. Of 13 languages spoken there, Shona has by far the most native speakers (10.6 million in a population of about 12.6 million). Before 1890, speech variation in this region formed what linguists call a "dialect chain." As one traveled from one locale to the next, one would encounter shifts or variation in

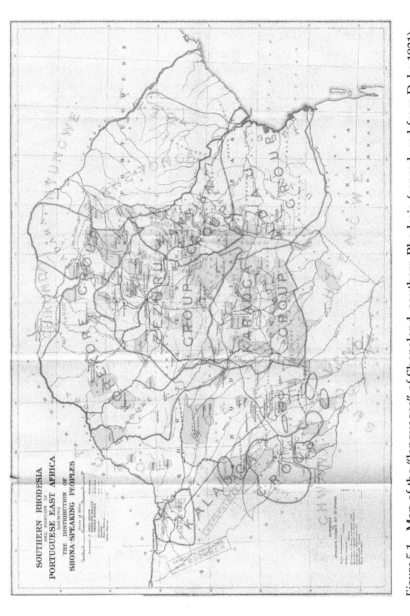

Figure 5.1   Map of the "languages" of Shonaland, southern Rhodesia (reproduced from Doke 1931).

the ways people spoke – pronunciation, grammar, word choice – which would not necessarily prevent members of neighboring communities from understanding each other. As one traveled, though, more such differences would be encountered, until eventually mutual intelligibility of speech would be lost. Before the coming of British colonialists to this region, these kinds of language difference had little importance as markers of social difference in comparison with attributes of kinship (affiliation with the Karanga or Manyika lineages of chiefly authority) and region (Korekore to the north, or the Zezuru highlands).

Emissaries of five different missionary groups came to this region in 1890: Anglicans from England, Catholics of two orders, Dutch Reformed Church missionaries, and American Methodists. Each was given its own "field of operation," demarcated by the colonial government which oversaw their work, and in each field were established churches and schools where the "local" language was taught with its own system of writing. Methodists, Anglicans, and Marianhill fathers, working in the east, devised a common writing system for what they called "chiManyika," but which "created rather than merely reflected" (Ranger 1989:127) the language of the "Manyika nation." Parallel projects in the other fields of operation produced other groups of Christian, colonial subjects who were literate in similarly compartmentalized languages, as mapped in Figure 5.1.

Two generations later the result of this work was described by a professional linguist, C. M. Doke, as follows:

> let us suppose England to be a heathen country. Four distinct Missionary Societies commence work, one among the Cockneys, one among the University class, one in Yorkshire, and one in Devonshire. Each produces a translation into the "local" vernacular, each further uses a different orthography and some split up their words into their component parts. What an enormous difference there would be between the four literary efforts; they would not be mutually understood. (Doke 1931:3–4)

Doke attributed this unfortunate situation to the amateurish work of untrained missionary linguists. It fell to him, a professional, to oversee the elimination of idiosyncratic uses of letters (in some cases as many as four) for a single speech sound. With a mandate from the government of Rhodesia, and financial support from the Carnegie Foundation, Doke resolved this Babel-like confusion in a meeting of representatives of the missionary groups to devise what was known as the Union Orthography.

In effect, the commission compromised on a writing system which corresponded to the speech of no single group or region. Herbert Chimhundu (1992), a historian of colonial Rhodesia, points out that the commission favored features of Zezuru, and secondarily Karanga and Manyika, as the "peak" dialects most strongly associated with Christianity, literacy, and colonial power. Ndau was less used, Korekore and Kalanga not at all.

Zezuru became the basic model for the Shona language in part because it was spoken natively in the environs of Salisbury (now Harare), the colonial (now national) center.[7] "Shona" was, to be sure, not a name known to its speakers, but "it [was] essential," Doke observed, "to use a definite name as a label for the whole cluster of groups. The fact that the people themselves do not acknowledge this name is really immaterial" (Doke 1931:3).

The Kalanga "language," for its part, was reclassified as a "dialect" of Ndebele, which was in fact an entirely separate language from a structural point of view, and not mutually intelligible with any "dialect" of Shona. Perhaps because the Kalanga region had no representatives at the committee meeting, though, its language and people were reallocated to the London Missionary Society's neighboring jurisdiction in Ndebele land.

When Doke came on the scene, then, no sense of Shona identity or language existed among speakers of these "dialects" (Ranger 1989:142), some of whom joined their missionaries to actively resist the reforms he instituted. They were defending not just habits of reading and writing, but internalized senses of sharedness of literacy and speech, faith and community. Beyond this, they were also resisting larger political and economic forces which were eroding the privileged social positions of scholarized elites by integrating the colony's different regions. Top-down linguistic "improvements" served the colonial state at a time when newly mobile migrant laborers left villages and agrarian economies behind for urban centers. They needed a language of wider contact in a modernizing colonial society, and it fell to the Doke Commission to "assemble dialects" of Shona by the work of "internal translation" into a common standard.[8]

Before long, though, the spread of Shona had its own naturalizing impact on speakers' senses of "ethnic" identity. "If in the 1930s no one in Makoni would have described themselves as 'Shona', by the late 1950s, when the nationalist movement came to the district, very many people thought in such terms" (Ranger 1989:143). Shona had by then become the symbol and instrument of an ethnic idea in modernizing Rhodesia. So, too, the new linguistic reality imposed by colonial policy was giving rise to a sense of distinctness among the Kalanga whose speech, once placed in the same territorial group as the Ndebele, had begun to change in ways which have now created a situation where its speakers cannot read the Shona Bible (Grimes 1984:302).

It is important to see that the establishment of "Unified Shona" did not return this region to some precolonial state of linguistic homogeneity which misguided missionaries had temporarily disrupted. Instead, it installed a new homogeneity conforming to the political, economic, and territorial logic of the colonial regime which oversaw those missionaries' fields of operations. When the logic of political control and economic advantage dictated the erosion of demarcations which the state had previously supported, language differences began to be effaced among members of what came to count as the larger community of "Shona." This new ethnolinguistic sharedness made language a central item in what Vail calls, referring to 19th century Africa more widely, the colonial "cultural package" (Vail 1989:11).

One from many: inventing origins in the Transvaal

Missionaries who sought to convert natives without destroying native cultures needed to develop place-linked images of linguistic purity, which were important intellectual resources in situations of great linguistic diversity. In one such region, the northern Transvaal, well-educated Swiss missionaries deployed philological images of the past like those sketched in chapter 4 to grapple with enormous complexity. South and east of Shonaland, on the borders of modern South Africa, Zimbabwe, and Mozambique, they encountered speakers of entirely different languages whom they were

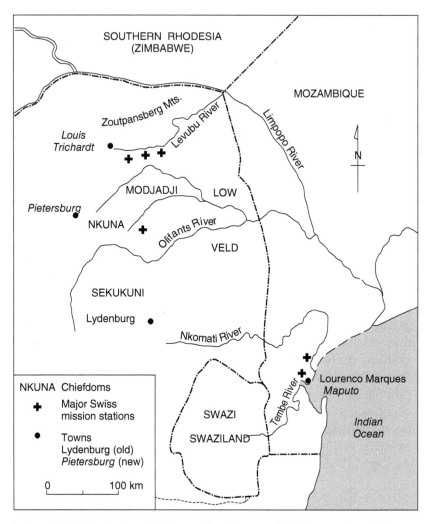

Figure 5.2 The Swiss mission to the Transvaal. Redrawn from Harries 1988. Reprinted by permission of Oxford University Press.

obliged, by the call of faith and the politics of missionary work, to convert to a unitary written language. So they partly described and partly created a print-literate language, Thonga, along with a speculative history of its speakers (Figure 5.2).

Paul Berthoud and Ernest Creux came to this area in 1872, sponsored by the Paris Missionary Society (PMS), to proselytize using the Sotho language they had learned during their earlier work among neighboring peoples. When they discovered that none of their prospective flock knew Sotho, they were – as good Protestants – reluctant to impose it as what would be an elitist mission language. Instead they undertook to learn "the local language," not knowing how many such languages were spoken in the region they took as their own. Historical records suggest that the linguistic diversity they encountered had developed recently when people moved inland from the coast of southeast Africa to escape the depredations of the Portugese. Living in scattered villages, sharing no allegiance to a common chief, and speaking no common tongue, they had little sense of community with each other or peoples already in the region.

The Swiss missionaries recognized early on the facts of linguistic diversity, but had strong economic and political reasons for using a single language in their work. Print materials were expensive, prohibitively so if they had to be produced in more than one language; linguistic diversity could weaken claims that theirs was a unitary field of operation, especially in the eyes of German missionaries who had already established jurisdiction over neighboring chiefdoms. The Swiss needed to operate as if there were comparable unity, linguistic and otherwise, among people in the territory they sought to claim.

To recover the unity they knew must be there, the missionaries focused on terms used by long-term residents for newcomers, whom they called *Gwamba* and *Thonga*. Though both words identified them as "outsiders," that is "not natives," each counted as evidence for Berthoud and Creux of underlying commonalities among them. The challenge, then, was to recover the linguistic grounds of that commonality and in so doing explain the historical forces which had eroded it so heavily. It fell to Paul Berthoud to partly describe and partly invent written images of the language he sometimes called Gwamba, and sometimes Thonga. This work was taken over by his brother Henri in 1882, who "systematized" the language in eight territorial divisions, although these "dialects" were, unfortunately, not mutually intelligible.

To reconstruct their underlying unity, Henri developed a philological image of linguistic descent like those discussed in chapters 3 and 4, together with a conjectural, Darwinistic history of ancient unity and subsequent dissolution. This theory, already widely recognized in educated European circles, led him to regard the Thonga people as inhabiting an early stage of social evolution like that of prefeudal Europe. He deduced "that foreign language forms, brought to the coastal areas by invaders in the fifteenth and sixteenth centuries, had mixed to varying degrees with the indigenous Thonga language" (Harries 1988:39).

With hindsight, the Berthoud brothers can be seen to have worked against the grain of historical and linguistic reality to create written Thonga and its history. But they succeeded in making them social facts among their literate converts. Once they had some intellectual purchase on local conditions of linguistic cultural difference, they could teach Thonga literacy and so also the Thonga language itself. By this process, over time, print literacy produced a language which a later missionary called "one of the most trustworthy and complete manifestations of [the Thonga nation's] mind," and "the oldest element in the life of the tribe . . . the great bond which bound the Thonga clans together in past centuries" (quoted in Harries 1988:39).

Philological images of the past also gave missionaries a proprietary relation to Thonga. It was theirs, as Edward Said might argue, because they created (or "systematized") it, but also because they monopolized its literate forms and uses. As Henri Berthoud put it, "their" print-based Thonga stood over and against the messy diversity of talk as a language does to its dialects, which "would be forced ipso facto into the position of patois destined to disappear with time" (quoted in Harries 1995:166).

A more complete rendition of the history of Thonga/Ronga would trace the results of regional conflicts among missionaries, centered on different written versions of the language, following the Berthoud brothers' pioneering work. Here it is enough to note that these conflicts centered on a common issue: which written images would represent language and identity in which regions. These developments gave rise to a community described by an American anthropologist in 1971 as "the Ronga tribe," which had "a delimited territory, a common language, common political structure, cultural unity; and an awareness of themselves as a distinct group" (Binford quoted in Harries 1995:171).

Missionaries' Positions

I have provided these simple sketches to show how missionaries were guided by European cultures of standardization as they devised linguistic descriptions with an eye to transmitting print-literate practices. In this way their linguistic work presupposed and helped to create unitary "languages" like Shona or Thonga/Ronga, but also broader part-for-whole relations reaching beyond writing and speech to language, identity, and territory. Philological images of the past were important, then, for more than reducing diversities of speech to writing: they helped missionaries conform to the exigencies of colonial power with "just so" stories which marginalized and eroded conditions of diversity in a colonial present.

Thus far I have largely passed over the different effects that missionaries' backgrounds and lives, or preterrains, could have on their work as linguists. These could be important, and real, as can be shown with one last example: a linguistic controversy among Catholic missionaries about the Congo. This can be read as being due partly to differences in their social biographies, senses of linguistic identity, and attitudes to colonial power. One is the Jesuit linguist Gaston Van Bulck whose 1948 linguistic map I presented in Figure 4.1 as a visual image for his Darwinian history of invasions and displacements of the weak by the strong. The other is Gustaaf Hulstaert, a linguist whose very different map of the same region (Figure 5.3) tells a very different story.

Hulstaert's map is strikingly simple and homogeneous in comparison with the one drawn up by Van Bulck, who distinguished seven distinct Mongo languages where Hulstaert maps one. Where Van Bulck portrayed scattered linguistic "enclaves," Hulstaert drew a picture of unfragmented linguistic sameness.

This simplicity was no reflection of ignorance. Van Bulck did his work in European libraries, but Hulstaert studied Mongo languages in the Congo from 1925, when his work for the Missionaries of the Sacred Heart eventually made him a "towering figure among missionary linguists" (Fabian 1986:81). These two pictures reflect disagreements less about linguistic facts than their meanings and relevance for Belgium's colonial agenda. Van Bulck's map is

Figure 5.3　Hulstaert's linguistic map of the Belgian Congo (reproduced from Hulstaert 1950).

grounded not just in a history of survival of the fittest, but the legitimacy of work by another superior power (Belgium) to impose civilizational authority on a disunited region. Because (as Schleicher showed) it is entirely natural for weak languages to die, this was an entirely natural result of Belgium's colonial project to educate (or scholarize) its subjects in more civilized but non-European languages of wider communication: Lingala and Swahili, which I discuss in the next chapter.

Hulstaert's map, on the other hand, reflects what Michael Meeuwis (1999) calls its author's "ideology of the natural." Hulstaert knew quite well that diverse dialects were spoken in this region, but saw in that diversity no evidence of the relative "weakness" and "strength" of languages. Minor differences, in his opinion, were viewed properly against the larger backdrop of natural, linguistic sharedness among the region's peoples. Though he acknowledged that a merging of some dialect clusters was appropriate, Hulstaert insisted that these languages represented the core of their speakers' identities, echoing Herder's philosophy of linguistic autonomy and authenticity. Hulstaert's map in this way counted as an argument against any colonial language of wider communication, which could only be an "anti-popular influence," "artificial and European," and a "rudimentary *passe-partout* language" which would "caus[e the native] civilization to regress in many degrees ... [after] an incalculable number of years of cultural evolution" (Hulstaert and DeBoeck, quoted in Meeuwis 1999:405–406).

The roots of Hulstaert's stance can be found not in his Catholic religion or Belgian nationality, but other parts of his preterrain. He was Flemish, from a region which was both linguistically distinct and politically and economically marginal in relation to Belgium's dominant, urban, Francophone population. He shared with many other Flemish speakers a strong sense of ethnic nationalism and of his native language as a crucial resource for resisting oppression. Hulstaert's life experience in this way resonated strongly with the conditions which animated romanticist philosophy and comparative philology, discussed in chapters 3 and 4, and with his brief against colonial encroachment on Congolese languages. Hulstaert's map can be read, then, as more than a rebuttal of claims by a fellow linguist. It reflects his cross-cultural and cross-linguistic identification with speakers of these "minority" languages, as he projected a sense of his own position among Europeans onto conditions on the other side of the colonial divide. (For discussion of other instances of such identification, see Steinmetz 2003.)

Conclusion

Whether or not they were talented, or inspired by the miracle of Pentecost, missionaries could only produce linguistic descriptions much simpler than the complex worlds of talk they found in their fields of operation. Because the work of linguistic conversion was founded in the work of selection, missionaries ran the risk of producing print-literate images which might count as what Franz Fanon called linguistic "effigies." This work was enabled, and constrained, by practices of print literacy and social imaginaries which extended beyond the dictates of faith and demands of power. Cultures of standardization lent missionaries' linguistic work authority and meaning not just in their eyes, or those of their converts, but in broader colonial regimes of power. Because they engaged with such an immediate and basic aspect of life, missionary linguists did some of the most intimate colonial work of "conceptualizing, inscribing, and interacting [with colonial subjects] on terms not of their own choosing" (Comaroff and Comaroff 1991:15).

By focusing here on the strategies and practices of this work, and some of its cumulative effects under colonial regimes, I have left to one side important and complex issues of how this work was received, resisted, and used by those whose speech the missionaries so partially described. Targets of conversion may not have rejected new versions of their languages, but by the same token they did not passively accept them, as missionaries to "the Shona" discovered. The capacity to devise print-literate images or practices of literacy sketched here did not translate into full control of the ways they were "transmitted" to colonial subjects: not just taught but learned, not just imposed but assimilated in ways missionaries did not necessarily recognize or condone.[9]

It has been useful here to present this work of reducing speech to writing as if it happened just from "above," not "below," and to consider in chapter 6 this more complex dynamic as it developed in two other projects of colonial linguistics and power. There I chart work which served projects of power as well as resistance, as linguists partly described and partly created languages which bridged the transition between colonial and postcolonial eras.

Notes to chapter 5

1 Readers may be reminded by this chapter's title of remarks which close George Steiner's *After Babel* (1975:470). It should be clear, though, that it serves here to name a very different range of concerns.

2 The biography of this hymn also offered a hopeful example for missionaries. The African evangelist Prophet William Wade Harris, who took his mission of conversion to tens of thousands of West Africans early in the 20th century, offers a native example of what many foreign missionaries sought to achieve. Harris was a Liberian who spoke English natively and, after a visitation by the angel Gabriel, began to preach in pidgin English, but with the Standard Authorized English Bible tucked under his arm. In this way he created Christian communities which are still vibrant today.

3 For the influence of this same strand of German mysticism on early nationalists, including Herder, see Greenfeld 1992.

4 A paradigmatic example of this dilemma has been very well described by James Clifford (1982) in his book about Maurice Leenhardt, a French missionary who spent years in Melanesia.

5 "Om een taal goed to leren moet men met het volk familjaar omgaan, en dit is bij sommige natiën niet anders mogelijk dan door hun godsdiesnt ann to nemen. En juist dit zou een genootschap dat van bigotterie leeft, als een doodzonde aanwitten."

6 The exception was Halhed's use of /oo/ for the "long vowel" at the ends of works like Hindu, which was too sedimented in English practices of literacy, it seemed, for even him to escape.

7 The representation or missionary groups and regions/dialects at the meeting was as follows:

Zezuru	Roman Catholic/Jesuits
Manyika	Roman Catholic, American Methodist, Anglican
Karanga	Dutch Reformed
Kalanga	London Missionary
Ndebele	London Missionary
Ndau	American Methodist
Korekore	None

8 Doke's work in fact was part of a much larger initiative begun in 1928 by the International Institute of African Languages and Cultures (1930), which devised a comprehensive phonetic alphabet for more than a dozen sub-Saharan African languages, including Shona.

9 Excellent sources for such work in sub-Saharan Africa are Stumpf's (1979) account of the politics of linguistics in Cameroon under three different colonial regimes, and Derek Peterson's *Creative writing* (2004), which describes the intellectual and political dynamics set in motion by missionaries and their linguistic work among the Gikuyu of colonial Kenya. See also Blommaert 2005 for a semiotically sophisticated account of this work.

Chapter 6

Colonial Linguists, (Proto)-National Languages

A language never spreads like a liquid, nor even like a disease or a rumor.

Johannes Fabian, *Language and colonial power* (1986:8)

The linguistic projects I sketch in this chapter might be called imperial, rather than colonial, to emphasize the ways they emerged and matured within the political and economic dynamics some called the New Imperialism. They differ from those discussed in chapter 5 most obviously in that they focused on languages which came to serve as languages of European power but were not native to Europeans: Swahili in the Belgian Congo, and Malay in the Netherlands East Indies (or NEI). Because both languages became central instruments of rule, linguists who engaged with them were also involved with the broader intellectual and ideological challenges of creating and legitimizing imperial power.

One ex-colonial officer, Leonard Woolf (husband of Virginia), used the phrase New Imperialism at the turn of the 20th century to describe the ways Europe's nations and the United States were imposing the will of their states "upon the world outside the State for the economic purposes of the world within the State" (Woolf 1919:16). Competition between imperial powers was shaped by a global economy as projects of power abroad came into closer alignment with national agendas and the dynamics of international commodity markets. Colonial subjects became increasingly important consumers of goods and targets of exploitation for labor on plantations, in mines, and so on. Technologies of communication and information created tighter administrative lines between peripheries and centers of empire, which needed more intimate forms of oversight over colonial subjects.

Imperial dynamics in this way produced another demand: colonial subjects who, after being suitably scholarized, could function as surrogates for Europeans in the infrastructures of colonial exploitation. These were new kinds of colonial subjects, members of a new dominant – yet still dominated – class, the kind of subaltern elite which made it possible for 60,000 Britons rule 300 million subjects in South Asia, and 30,000 Dutch to oversee some 70 million "natives" (in Dutch, *inlanders*) in the NEI. In 1916 the Belgian Ministry of Colonies similarly began to pressure functionaries in the Congo to begin creating a class of "black clerks and craftsmen" to replace "lower-echelon white personnel who were very expensive and produced mediocre results" (Fabian 1986:50).

As the New Imperialism gave rise to new institutional hierarchies among colonial subjects, it also created hierarchies of languages, which had new places and effects on senses of social identity. In the British and French empires, colonial subjects were commonly educated in their masters' national, native languages. But in the Belgian Congo and the NEI, other hierarchies were created as Europeans and non-Europeans alike learned non-native, non-European languages of power as what the French called a "vehicular language" (*langue véhiculaire*), the Germans a "language of unity" (*Einheitsprache*), and the English a "language of wider communication" (a phrase I discuss below). Such languages came to the fore in the late colonial era in response to requirements of power much like those served by Nahuatl in 16th century Mexico.

Swahili was the language of wider communication (or LWC) that Van Bulck saw as a civilizing force which would drive out weaker languages (discussed in chapter 4), and which Hulstaert regarded with deep suspicion for the same reason (discussed in chapter 5). Because Johannes Fabian likewise recognized its importance as an object of imperial knowledge and instrument of imperial rule, his account of Swahili's development, *Language and colonial power*, is also a groundbreaking account of the contradictions and dilemmas of empire in the Congo. Drawing on his critical reading of this work of imperial linguistics, I present here similar work by

Dutch linguists which had Malay as its object, tracing conundrums of language and human difference which Dutch imperialists were no more able to avoid, resolve, or fully stabilize than their Belgian counterparts.

First I describe the philological images of the past and strategies of selection which linguists in the NEI, like their counterparts elsewhere, used to partly describe and partly create an imperial Malay. Unlike colonial linguists in many other places, though, they were not just technicians of literacy who reduced an unruly diversity to a unitary written image. They operated also as technocrats of education, extending their custodial relation beyond that written image to secular projects of power, rather than religious conversion.

The second important issue here is how their technical and technocratic work shaped categories of linguistic and social difference which came into play when the languages used in zones of colonial contact were spoken non-natively on both sides of the imperial divide. In this respect, social histories and forms of use of both Swahili and Malay embodied what Cooper and Stoler (1997) have called the "tensions of empire." Each language was designed as a way to absorb colonialized speakers into a project of civilization, but also to impose on them projects of power and exploitation; each served to "project outward [European] ways of understanding the world, [but also] to demarcate colonizer from colonized, civilized from primitive, core from periphery" (Cooper 2005:4). Tracing this tension as it played out in the politics of Malay helps to chart that language's development into an instrument for protonational resistance to the imperial power it originally served.

This leads to the third major concern in this chapter: effects of work by colonial linguists that outran their intent, which neither they nor other imperial officials could fully control or recognize. Colonial subjects pirated "their" languages for purposes of their own, showing how teaching a language is a bit like providing information or money: once given, the giver loses control of the ways they are used. As empires' custodial relations to Malay and Swahili were eroded by communities of subaltern speakers, those languages could come to embody newer, increasingly public versions of protonational, anti-imperial identities.

With these three broad issues in mind, I chart Malay's development in the space between imperial institutions and interests on one hand, and the dynamics of community solidarity and conflict on the other. Its shifting uses as a communicative conduit, and meanings as a symbol of identity, can be articulated with Fabian's observation about Swahili, quoted at the head of this chapter. I foreground "language spread" as a label which is not just oversimple, but because its simplicity makes it ideologically useful for imaginaries of empire. In this way, I suggest, these two projects of imperial linguistics were founded on and helped make "natural" a range of metaphors of social and linguistic change –osmotic flow, quasi-mechanical replication, biological reproduction, etc. – which are still in use to describe and disguise the workings of power through language.

Imperial Ideologies of Language Difference

As the New Imperialism created tighter relations between metropolitan centers and peripheries of imperial power, language policies abroad were indirectly shaped by ideologies of language and national identity in Europe. This interplay between national ideology and imperial policy can be read from controversies which emerged when Prussia began the work of overtaking its imperial neighbors, not long after the science of language I sketched in chapter 4 reached the apex of its prestige and influence.

As a latecomer to the club of colonial powers, Prussia's imperial ambitions were formally ratified by the other participants at the Berlin West Africa Conference in 1885. Zeal for colonial projects ran strong in several sectors of Prussian society, including those which had long supported religious missions. Friedrich Fabri, a minister and administrator of missions to Africa, argued in an influential 1859 book that Africans were fit colonial subjects because they had inherited the curse placed on their forebear, Ham, for his part in building of the tower of Babel. Twenty years later he argued that Prussia's troubled economy could be helped by forming economic colonies (*Handelskolonien*) in Samoa, New Guinea, North Borneo, Formosa, Madagascar, and Central Africa (Fabri 1998[1879]).

Identity-linked ideologies of German language and nation discussed in chapter 4, could only be transposed with difficulty to colonial zones of contact, and communication across lines of racial difference. On the one hand Germans believed, Mazrui suggests, "that no African was good enough to speak the German language" (1975:142) thanks to their "ideology of the natural," to recall Meeuwis' phrase from chapter 5. But this created a practical dilemma for colonial agents who needed communicative conduits across colonial territory, and within colonial institutions.

> German colonial authorities at first unanimously [took] the view that the learning of the German language by the African population had to be carried out as quickly as possible as the most expedient way of achieving education in the spirit of "Germanism" of the imperialist type and of making the colonies a safe field for exploitation by German monopoly capital." (Mehnert 1973:384)

But nativist senses of linguistic identity caused many to balk at the prospect of "giving" German to their native subjects. The German Evangelist Missionary Societies called on Prussia in 1897 to avoid creating a "demanding, easily inflamed and educated proletariat due to the spread of European languages" (quoted in Mehnert 1973:388). Seven years later members of this same committee reiterated that knowledge of German was

> a danger for the colony since it leads to the development of a conceited, demanding, and easily dissatisfied race . . . [I]n possession of the language of the Europeans, [the colonized] feel tempted to consider themselves as equal to them. . . . With the understanding of the language of the foreigner, his personal authority also vanishes for ever. (Quoted in Mehnert 1973:391)

The prospect of a native yet German-speaking community was worrisome enough to Carl Meinhof, the eminent Africanist I discussed in chapter 5, that he presented to the Colonial Conference of 1905 a strategic negative example. The spread of English in South Africa, he argued, was causing the "rising of several tribes [which before] could not be prepared on account of the language frontiers and tribal differences" (quoted in Mehnert 1973:389).

Inheritors of Herder's tradition may have feared the dislocating, disordering effects of their language on the natural state of their subjects, but the French and English had no such qualms. They "spread" their languages as symbols of civilization, and as instruments of rule. The French regarded no African as being of any worth until he or she spoke French, Ali Mazrui suggests, because the spread of their language abroad (*la Francophonie*) extended the same assimilationist policies being pursued at home, transforming peasants into French-speaking citizens of the Republic.[1] Colonial subjects in the empire were that part of "a white man's burden . . . whose first conquests were to be right at home" (Weber 1976:73).

British imperial language policy coalesced formally and famously with the victory of the so-called Anglicists over the orientalists in the 1835 debate on the future of India. (See Trautmann 1997 for further discussion.) The colonial regime, as Thomas Macaulay wrote in his (in)famous "Minute on Indian education," was instructed to make English a means for "uplifting" the Indian people, creating an Anglophone elite which would be "Indian in blood and colour, but English in taste, in opinions, in morals, and in intellect (Macaulay 1972[1835]:249).[2]

Belgium and the Netherlands stand apart from Europe's other imperial powers in two obvious ways. Both were small countries which were really interstitial on the political landscape, positions indirectly reflected by the fact that neither possessed a distinctive, unitary national language of its own. Flemish was spoken "natively" in Belgium, but only by members of the politically and economically marginal ethnic group of which Hulstaert was a member. Dutch, which I discuss below, was spoken as a range of dialects which had strong resemblances to dialects of German on the Netherlands' eastern border.

When these two tiny nations came into possession of enormous, linguistically diverse, imperial territories much larger than their own countries, they elected to withhold access to "their" languages from almost all their colonial subjects. Adopting the stance urged on the Germans by Meinhof, they made language difference a correlate of "social distance . . . in order to know who was the ruler and who was the ruled" (Mazrui and Kazungu quoted in Mkangi 1985:334). From an ideological point of view, nativeness of knowledge made speech a constant, embodied mark of the collective difference of colonial subjects from themselves. Because talk was self-evidently exemplary of identity, minor differences in accent and intonation could be "natural" and naturalizing marks of differ-ence and deficiency.

From a technocratic point of view, it seems that the ideological was ascendant over the practical, because European languages were already institutionally grounded in the print-literate practices which Europeans needed to develop for Swahili and Malay to serve as efficient means of communication, and as "second" languages learned and spoken in the absence of native, "exem-plary" speakers. To discuss the larger political and cultural implications of this important circumstance, it is useful to think of Swahili and Malay not as having been spoken *non-natively* (like French by an African or English by an Indian) but *un-natively*: in the absence of native-speaking reference points. This label helps to examine the importance of institutions and practices of literacy which made it possible for Malay and Swahili to be described and used as un-native, non-European languages of wider communication.

Languages of Wider Communication

To frame the issues confronting imperial technocrats in the linguis-tically diverse Congo and NEI, it is useful to draw on more recent discussion of challenges faced by their postcolonial Cold War suc-cessors as "language problems of developing nations." (See, for instance, Fishman et al. 1968.) Before and after the end of the im-perial era, a common solution was to "superpose," or introduce from above, literate forms of European languages of power, through the work of suitably scholarized members of otherwise linguisti-cally distinct populations. I noted in chapter 5 that during the impe-rial era this educational work fell to missionaries in some colonies, whether they wished to do it or not. This was a strong reason for colonial regimes to require that missionaries be from the home nation, and native speakers of the national language.

Postcolonial framings of these issues center on "development," but during the imperial era civilizational images were elaborated by linguists with an older, universalist teleology of progress and modernity. This can be read from the work of the well-known lin-guist Otto Jespersen, a Dane with no national investment in any imperial project, but a strong intellectual investment in Darwinian history.

Jespersen was born in 1860, the year after Darwin's *Origin of species* was published, a man of his times steeped in social Darwinism before publishing his first philological treatise, *Progress in language* (1894). In this he showed his adeptness in the time-honored academic tradition of honoring, critiquing, and then appropriating ideas (and prestige) from a major intellectual ancestor, in his case August Schleicher. Jespersen used the evolutionary doctrine of uniformitarianism to develop more rigorous analogies between linguistic and natural history than Schleicher did. If forces of change operate uniformly over time in the domain of language as well as nature, Jespersen argued, then deep linguistic history can be excavated with the guidance of more accessible, "shallower" stages of history. In this way Jespersen bracketed the idea that the present state of a language depends crucially on its formative conditions of origin, and focused instead on its susceptibility to universal forces of change.

Jespersen also criticized Schleicher's lack of "a rational basis for determining the relative value or merit of different languages." Invoking their common ancestor, Wilhelm von Humboldt, Jespersen observed that "language means speaking, and that speaking means action on the part of a human being to make himself understood by somebody else," and so concluded "that language ranks highest which goes farthest in the art of accomplishing much with little means, or, in other words, which is able to express the greatest amount of meaning with the simplest mechanism" (Jespersen 1894:13).

Jespersen's utilitarian metric for gauging progress in language was innovative in that he centered on a much narrower, more abstract sense of "meaning" than had Herder, von Humboldt, or many others attuned to expressive authenticity. Jespersen, like many of his intellectual contemporaries, accounted for "meaning" as a matter of how elements of languages serve to "pick out" and characterize things spoken of in the world. When speech is a matter of identifying things with acts of reference, and characterizing them with acts of predication, then its efficiency can be calculated as a ratio between properties of linguistic form ("mechanism") and content ("amount of meaning").

This jump from a romanticist to a positivist view of language allowed Jespersen to compare languages and their stages of development, as he showed with one of Schleicher's own examples: the historical development of modern English *had* from Gothic *habaidêdeima*:

> The English form is preferable, on the principle that any one who has to choose between walking one mile or four miles will, other things being equal, prefer the shorter cut. . . . The English form saves a considerable amount of brain work to all English-speaking people, and especially to every child learning the language. (Jespersen 1894: 19–20)

With vague aesthetic considerations set aside, Jespersen turned the question of linguistic development on its head: "[t]he so-called full and rich forms of the ancient languages are not a beauty but a deformity" (Jespersen 1894:14). This becomes clear in the linguistic present and "analytic structures" of modern European languages, which mark their "unimpeachable superiority over the earlier stages of the same languages."

Jespersen continued to demonstrate their superiority in *Language; its nature, development and origin*, published in 1922, when he was one of the best known linguists in the world. Taking up the perennial question of "lines of development" of speech, he drew on languages of "barbarous races" which are rich in words for particulars, but not for broader categories which subsume them. Knowingly or not, he echoed Herder's comments on Arabic 140 years earlier, with examples from the language of the aboriginals of Tasmania – already exterminated, along with their language – which offered no general word for "tree" but plentiful names for specific varieties of tree (gum-tree, wattle-tree, etc.) (Jespersen 1964[1922]:429). Jespersen gave a new accent to old observations and what was by then common knowledge: primitiveness was evident in languages which prevented speakers from seeing the abstract woods for the concrete trees.[3]

Jespersen's vision of "progress" in language paralleled work among philosophers of language who were modeling languages as "referential systems sensitive to nature and blind to society" (Gellner 1994:51). (This was the project rejected by Wittgenstein which I noted in chapter 1.) Together, linguists and philosophers could justify a utilitarian ideal of language uniformly distributed across space, groups, and institutions, and a maximally efficient conduit for information – identifying and characterizing things – independently from other kinds of shared knowledge. Messages are more autonomous when the conventions of languages are established independently of communities and locales.

There is an ideological connection between this conception of language and the workings of empire which is important enough to be discussed briefly with an eye to the work of Ernest Gellner, a philosopher of language and social change. Gellner argues that modern nations need to "spread" languages through educational infrastructures and practices of print literacy. Such work must be coordinated by a centralizing state, he further asserts, so that people who would otherwise never know each other all undergo parallel processes of what he calls "exo-socialization [and] exo-education." This makes it possible for them to communicate despite differences between the "local intimate units" of which they are members (Gellner 1983:38).

Gellner framed this argument to account for the rise of modern nations, but it fits well the logic of work by colonial regimes to "spread" the languages of interest here. Malay and Swahili had to be made into what Europe's languages already were, what Gellner calls "school-mediated, academy-supervised idiom[s] codified for the requirements of reasonably precise bureaucratic and technological communication" (Gellner 1983:57). Only then could they count as what Jespersen would have recognized as products and instruments of genuine progress.

I emphasize these as background assumptions for the work of "spreading" a language of imperial power, and making plausible, part-for-whole linkages between forms of language on one hand, and conditions of modernity on the other. There is an important break with romanticist tradition here, because these imperial projects were designed, "top down," to distribute linguistic knowledge uniformly across individuals, as if the work of producing linguistic *sameness* need have no effects on senses of social *sharedness*. This partialness of vision can be traced in the history of Dutch imperial efforts to describe and "spread" Malay as "their" language of wider communication.

From Pidgin to Language: Malay People, Malay Speakers

From a technocrat's point of view, Swahili and Malay might seem poor candidates for languages of wider communication because they require more "initial inputs" than European languages. Europeans who encountered these ways of speech without any suitable practices of literacy – although both languages were in fact written by native speakers with Arabic-derived scripts – needed alphabets suitable for institutionally print-literate practices. Only then could Malay "spread" across colonial territory and otherwise diverse populations.

Swahili presented challenges to the Belgians, Fabian argues, which can be read from the colonial archive of linguistic work to reduce it to alphabetic writing. Drawing on the philological tradition I discussed in chapters 4 and 5, linguists created an image of what they assumed to have been a "pure" Swahili which originated, conveniently for their own purposes, outside their domain: among native speakers living as far away as the east coast of Africa and on the island of Zanzibar. This philological displacement of the language's origin helped to cement the Belgians' custodial relation to Swahili, cutting it off from what would otherwise be its dangerous associations with Islam.

At the same time, linguists used strategies of selection, much like missionaries discussed in chapter 5, to bypass messy pluralities of talk in Swahili in different colonial communities. Unitary images of "their" Swahili helped marginalize other versions which Europeans never used or understood, but which were nonetheless intimate parts of the lives of some of their subjects.[4]

Parallel work partly described and partly created Malay as a print-literate language of wider communication (LWC) in the NEI, which covered as much of the globe as the United States, and was home to millions of speakers of hundreds of native languages. By 1930, Malay was fully officialized, even though it was spoken natively by a tiny fraction of the colonial population, under the name *bahasa Melayu* in that language. "Malaysian" (*bahasa Malaysia*) now refers to both native and official dialects of so-called indigenous peoples of the nation-state of Malaysia (i.e., non-Chinese,

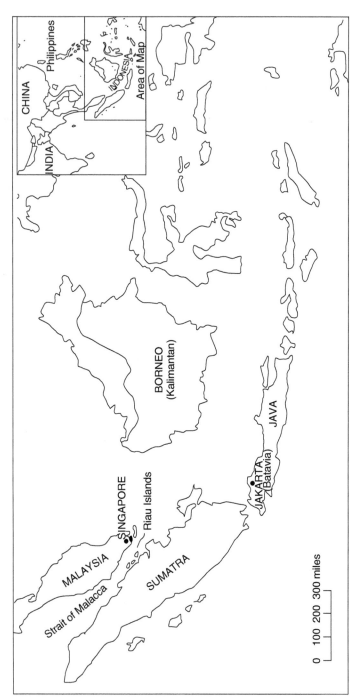

Figure 6.1   Map of Indonesia, the Netherlands East Indies (NEI) (redrawn from Stoler 1985).

non-Indian, *bumiputra*).[5] "Indonesian" (*bahasa Indonesia*) now names the official language of the nation-state which emerged from much of the territory of the former NEI, still spoken un-natively by most citizens.

In the 1600s, Portuguese explorers and traders had encountered *bahasa Melayu* as a "trade language," "market language," or non-native LWC needed to do business as far east as the coast of India and as far north, by some accounts, as Japan. In the Straits of Malacca they found people who wrote Malay with an Arabic-based script, and spoke it as one of the "cultured languages of the world . . . [the] language of educated people, from the flooding Indus to China and Japan, and in most of the Eastern islands, much like Latin in our Europe" (Jean-Baptiste Tavernier 1605 quoted in Werndly 1736:xxxvii).

Bahasa Melayu was bound to no sense of ethnic or national identity among these speakers, whose primary allegiances were to Islam and the kingdom of Melaka. The Portuguese defeat of that kingdom caused a diaspora of "Malays" to trading ports on coasts of the many neighboring islands in the early 16th century (Maier 1993:45). So by the time the Swiss linguist Werndly wrote his Malay grammar in 1736, Malay was spoken in ports which had become important for the Dutch, who had forced the Portuguese out of the area and monopolized the lucrative spice trade.

Extensive experience had taught the Dutch that there were two basically different kinds of Malay:

> High Malay, which is spoken among the high-ranking persons at the Courts and is used in matters pertaining to the Mohammaden religion; and Low Malay or Pasar, the Market Malay spoken as the everyday language in the community. (Valentijn 1724–1726 II-1:244)

Malay's doubleness was to become a recurring theme in a centuries-long controversy among traders, military men, and missionaries: what language would best serve their purposes – Dutch, High Malay, or some variety of Low Malay (see Hoffman 1979)? Colonial expansion only complicated this question as the Dutch created new zones of colonial contact in pursuit of new interests and projects.

From these colonial adventures also arose a Creole colonial community of native speakers of yet another variety of Malay. In the 16th century, Dutch operations were centered in the trading entrepot called Batavia on Java's northwest coast (now Jakarta, Indonesia's capital). The dominant segment of this polyglot Creole community had developed earlier when Portuguese traders and "native" women had "creole" or "mestizo" children. These children, and later those of Dutch men and their native or mestizo wives and concubines, grew up as native speakers of Portuguese and Malay dialects. One traveler noted late in the 16th century that "when they reach adulthood they can scarcely speak a word of Dutch decently, far less maintain a rational conversation without mixing many words of pidgin Portuguese in it" (N. De Graaff quoted in Taylor 1983:43).

By the 18th century, though, Dutch colonial interests had shifted to the fertile lands of central Java, and required intensive, sustained contact with the Javanese elite I mentioned in chapter 3. These were "natives" distinguished not only by their Kawi literary tradition, but a complex system of linguistic politesse in their spoken language.[6]

The nuanced styles of Javanese speech, keyed to finely differentiated ranks and statuses, created problematic interactional politics in zones of colonial contact which Europeans elsewhere in the world might have recognized. On one hand, foreigners who incorrectly used those styles could offend just those powerful native elites to whom the most deference was owed, and whose support was most needed. On the other hand, ignorance of those niceties could be taken as license by native inferiors to show the Dutch less respect than was their due. As William Gilchrist, the British student of Hindustani I mentioned in chapter 4, observed: "[t]he insult of the use of a familiar form by the servant to the sahib was not just a personal insult but had a much greater consequence of the loss of dignity for his country and nation" (quoted in Cohn 1996b:43).

To avoid both these interactional pitfalls, and the need to teach Dutch to the Javanese, the colonialists had recourse to Malay, such as they knew it, to communicate across the colonial divide. From the early 18th to the late 19th century, the Dutch satisfied themselves with *ad hoc*, improvised communication in Malay, preferring it, as one linguist acidly noted, in ways "inversely proportional to their knowledge of the language" (Heinrich Kern quoted in Groeneboer 1998:142). These improvised modes of un-native speech came to have a name which reflected its home in zones of colonial contact: "service Malay" (*dienstMaleisch*).

Imperial malaise

Fabian's careful study revealed a broad contrast between two types of Swahili communication which are unequally described in the colonial archive. "Vertical" communication occurred in "highly structured and hierarchical interaction" (Fabian 1986:108), while "horizontal" communication went on within subaltern communities, usually beyond colonial oversight. Un-native service Malay, used but looked down on by Dutch and Javanese alike, emerged in contexts of "vertical communication" as a barely adequate means for doing business across constantly patrolled borders of colonial difference. But as colonial society developed along with increasingly differentiated zones of contact, a plurality of needs for "horizontal communication" gave rise to the plurality of Malays, reflected in the 30 or so labels which were in use by the end of the 19th century: "barracks Malay," "market Malay," "service Malay," etc.

These Malays were basically similar in grammar and lexicon, but they differed depending on the zones of contact in which they served. A "loose network of differences and tensions" came to be mirrored in the ways these Malays were spoken "in the shadow of a center . . . [which was] strong enough to impose some kind of political and economic unity but too weak to impose a distinct cultural hegemony" (Maier 1993:46).

Over the course of the 19th century, a burgeoning mercantile economy and urban society also gave rise to print-literate Malay, used in newspapers written in the Roman alphabet for a heterogeneous readership. Newspapers were written in a distinctly "low" Malay because "high" varieties of the language – associated in any event with Arabic practices of literacy – differed too much from the speech of prospective readers to be understood easily, including those in the important ethnic Chinese market (Adam 1995:50).

This new Malay – vernacular yet literate, used widely in imperial society, yet not under the control of imperial authorities – posed an

indirect but real threat to the NEI government. This undomesti-
cated, quasi-public language arose from dynamics which profited
the empire but which it could not fully govern. Beyond this was
another social problem with a linguistic face: a linguistically hybrid
"mestizo" or Creole community whose members were called Indo-
Europeans, or Indos for short. Some Indos were "pure blood" children of Europeans born in the Indies or outside the Netherlands,
but living in the NEI and owing it allegiance as a "second father-
land" (Stoler 2002:106).

More problematic were interracial Indo descendants of (mostly)
Dutch men, who were numerous enough that by 1924 some 10,000
had joined an official group called the *Indo-Europeesch Verbond*.
Racially interstitial Indos were not regarded as a political threat to
the colonial regime; they "could neither enlist a popular constituency nor dissociate from [a] strong identification with the
European-born Dutch elite" (Stoler 2002:107). But just as their bodies
were undeniable physical evidence of hybridity, which was problematic for a racial ideology of empire, so too their distinctive ways
of speaking native Malay set them off as socially hybrid. It posi-
tioned Indos well, in fact, for important roles in the burgeoning
public press, thanks to "their knowledge of Low Malay or Javanese
and their reputed familiarity with Indonesian and with other
Foreign Orientals" (Adam 1995:44).

By the 1890s "the Indo problem" was so acute that the colonial
regime took steps to address their troublesome linguistic hybridity
with educational programs designed to educate young Indos into
correct use of "their" Dutch language. But these programs neither
removed telling traces of Malayness from their Dutch speech – at
least as far as the Dutch from the Netherlands, the *totok*, were
concerned – nor induced them to renounce their own Malay, called
Petjo. Distinguished by a heavy admixture of Dutch, *Petjo* was the
linguistic emblem of a hybrid identity, and for the imperial regime
what one linguist called "the one great enemy of the social-
economic development of the Indo population group" (Fokker
1891:83 quoted in Hoffman 1979:84).

This proliferation of varieties of Malay – serving imperial interests and threatening imperial authority – gave impetus to the project
of colonial linguistics which was designed to finally establish
governmental authority in this sphere of social life. The work of

"describing" Malay in the NEI, like Swahili in the Congo, counted in part as a response to social tensions that the language of Malay embodied, and the challenge it represented to colonial racial hierarchies.

Imperial Malays

Over most of the 19th century, Dutch imperialists, like their Belgian counterparts, managed without a "public register or form of discourse" (Fabian 1986:139) that also counted as "theirs." As early as the 1820s, some had recognized their need for institutional purchase on Malay, and sought to develop a "self-consciously proprietorial attitude of didactic Dutch scholarship towards the [Malay] language" (Hoffman 1979:78). Three generations later, though, Dutch linguists were still calling for a Malay which could be "an identical idiom . . . understood and spoken everywhere" (Fokker 1891 quoted in Hoffman 1979:84–85).

In 1855 the colonial government commissioned a Malay–Dutch dictionary from the linguist H. von de Wall, which he based on research in the Riau islands, in the straits of Malacca, and on the Malay peninsula. The work he left unfinished at his death passed to H. N. van der Tuuk, the linguist whose rueful remarks on the work of translating the Batak language I quoted in chapter 4. He completed von de Wall's work in 1877, but not without bitter complaints about the deficiencies resulting from his predecessor's reliance on spoken Malay, and his lack of reference to literary sources.

Van der Tuuk, the Indo son of a Dutch official and Eurasian wife, had traveled to Holland to study law but threw it over for philology. Though he became well known in his own time for groundbreaking studies of a range of languages in the NEI, he brought a lifelong concern for Malay, philological expertise, and an acid writing style to the problem of what he called the "babble" language (*brabbeltaal*) of Low Malay. This "demeaned officials when they spoke it, and could not elevate natives because it did not speak to their hearts in their language" (Grijns 1996:369).

Van der Tuuk criticized his colleague's dictionary as a philologist who took Bopp and Grimm as his "heroes in the field" (Teeuw 1971: xviii). He grounded his own image of a "general, cultured Malay" (in Dutch, *algemeen beschaafd Maleis*) in the philological notion that "every language [is] more or less a ruin, in which the plan of the architect cannot be discovered, until one has learned to supply from other works by the same hand what is missing in order to grasp the original design" (Grijns 1996:359). Van der Tuuk may have been unusual as a philologist who sought out intimate contact with speakers of the languages he studied, but rooted his descriptions in the philological, text-centered methods of reconstruction described in chapter 3. So fundamental were written materials for van der Tuuk's methods that if texts were not available he would induce literate natives to commit some of their language to writing for him to study (Teeuw 1971:xx–xxxiv).

Van der Tuuk was not the linguist who finally determined the forms of "general, cultured Malay," but his reputation and trenchant opinions did help induce the government to deal once and for all with "the Malay question." Charles van Ophuijsen – another child of the Indies, trained in philology and several Asian languages in the Netherlands – was commissioned in 1908 to devise a Malay orthography and grammar. He followed in von de Wall's footsteps to Sumatra and the Riau islands, but also worked "abroad" – which is to say beyond Dutch imperial territory – in the Malay peninsula and Singapore.

In 1910 van Ophuijsen's Malay grammar was published in Holland to educate candidates for colonial officialdom. In the introduction, he explained why the Malay of the Riau islands was the "best":

> In our country [the Netherlands] a variety of dialects are found which show considerable variation; their influence cannot be denied, even in speech of civilized people. Nonetheless we speak of one Dutch language, and regard it as the language of the Dutch people as a whole, even if it originally was only a dialect which has come to overshadow other regional ways of speaking, because it came to be means of literary and other kinds of writing.
>
> So it is also with Malay.
>
> Among the various dialects, Malays – and they are after all the only qualified judges – give priority to that dialect spoken in Johor, a part of Malacca, in the Riau Lingga Archipelago. . . . This so-called Riau or Johor Malay, in which the greater part of the literature is written will be dealt with in this work. (Van Ophuijsen 1910:2)

Van Ophuijsen's parallel between standard Dutch (called in Dutch *Algemeen Beschaavd Nederlands*) and "his" Malay is interesting because, according to Bruce Donaldson (1983:108), standard Dutch was never natively spoken in any region of the Netherlands. It seems to have emerged, rather, from a process rather like that used by Doke to produce the "Shona language" of Rhodesia, discussed in chapter 5. It was the product of a committee charged by state authority to devise a uniform orthography for a related group of dialects. Early 17th century controversy over Calvinist doctrine induced leading figures in the northern part of the region to commission a new translation of the Bible, which would bear none of the distinctive traits of speech heard to the south. But this required accommodating differences between the dozen or so dialects spoken in the north. The committee undertook this work by making concessions here and there to "assemble" those dialects in a text-based image of linguistic unity which reflected all partly, but none entirely.

Whether or not van Ophuijsen knew this history, he did his own work with recourse to philological images of pure texts and pure forms. Like the missionary linguists I described in chapter 5, philology licensed his part-for-whole substitutions between letter and voice, simple past and complex present, formal styles and living diversities of talk. But van Ophuijsen's written Malay was part of a print-centered, state-sponsored project enabled by an "extraordinary symbiosis of scholarship with the metropolitan politics of a colonizing state" (Hoffman 1973:22).

Imperial institutions and ideology strengthened the NEI state's custodial relation to Malay enough that some colonial subjects began to call it, in one or another of its varieties, *bahasa Belanda* (literally, "Dutch language") rather than *bahasa Melayu* (Maier 1993:57). This label reflects the success of government efforts to establish Malay as a symbol of its power, and an instrument of its institutions. A "long-term project to homogenize and unify Malay" (Maier 1993:55) was feasible precisely because it was artificial, or "stiff" (Teeuw 1973:120), thanks to the ways it could be "spread" along with literacy. The state publishing house (Balai Pustaka) supplied reading materials in "good" Malay (as well as major ethnic languages) for "a new class of potential readers, with different living and reading habits, with different expectations with regard to books, based on their school experiences" (Teeuw 1973:112). "These language officers" (called in Dutch *taalambtenaren*) practiced a "unique combination . . . of . . . pure [linguistic] science and applied science oriented to social needs" (Teeuw 1973:112) as they oversaw Balai Pustaka publications of fiction, poetry, and criticism which muted Islamic and ethnic Chinese themes in favor of visions of modernity, progress, and humanism.

Diglossic hierarchies

Van Ophuijsen reduced Malay to alphabetic writing by appropriating and fixing what Fabian, describing the colonial linguistics of Swahili, called "chains of hierarchical relations" (1986:4). In both colonial projects, Latin orthographies came into ascendance over Arabic scripts, representing the authority of colonial regimes over politically dangerous Islam. But neither print-based language could gain purchase in a colonial society at large unless it came to be recognized as an authoritative reference point, standing apart from and "above" a wide range of dialects.

From the apex and center of imperial power, "general, cultured Malay" could be viewed as part of the work of linguistic progress Jespersen spelled out with his refined social Darwinism. The science of language promoted "progress" in Malay as a uniform medium for communicating information (or "content") in efficient, context-free "forms." At once like and inferior to European languages, it was ideologically grounded in what Philip Abrams (1988[1977]:58) calls a state idea, and institutionally grounded in a state system. Its written images made the empire's modernity concrete and legible in "a palpable nexus of practice and institutional structure." In these two ways Malay, like Swahili, served in what Fabian calls "professional routines and ideological stereotypes" which insulated simple, literate images from "the subversive effects of close human interaction" (Fabian 1986:131).

But the view was very different from other places in colonial society. At the margins of colonial power and oversight – on the street and in the market, on the dock and in the neighborhood – Malay continued to be a messy plurality of ways of talking. What Fabian calls the "subversive effects of . . . human interaction" allowed Malay vernaculars to coalesce in "horizontal" communication beyond state oversight.

So the work of colonial linguistics in the NEI had as one side effect a broad linguistic asymmetry between print-literate and "vernacular" Malays. This kind of durable, hierarchical relation, reproduced over time and across generations, has come to be called "diglossic" in the field of sociolinguistics. In the 1950s, Charles Ferguson's studies of Arabic led him to propose *diglossia* as a descriptive term for societies which use two varieties of a single language, "low" and "high" (Ferguson 1959). Since then the term has been broadened to refer to similar relations existing between distinct languages: Alcuin's Europe can be called diglossic because unitary Latin, the Truth language of Christianity, stood over and against a plurality of local vernaculars; the "spread" of Nahuatl's "lordly speech" in Mexico could likewise be classified as the "superposition" of the literate "high" form, once friars appropriated it for their own purposes. Here I can call Malay in the colonial NEI broadly diglossic, in the sense of the word set out by Ralph Fasold (1984:53).

This kind of diglossia exists when, in addition to some variety of language learned first and in informal situations, another relatively highly valued variety of language is learned not in the home but later, more consciously, through formal education, and is used in situations perceived as more formal and guarded. The "high" variety is in one way or other associated with institutions of authority (religious, political, economic, etc.) and, quite often, with practices of literacy which shape its transmission. So colonial regimes that imposed non-native, literacy-related languages on colonial subjects sought to create diglossic situations by transmitting "high" language varieties to segments of the colonized population.

Within dominant segments of society, then, High Malay could be understood, thanks to the work of philologists, as the "better," "real" language and could stand, part-for-whole, for the quotidian realities of Malay which included everyday, "low" talk in society at large. But these print-based, school-supported notions of "correctness" lacked purchase in diverse communities of colonial subjects, where communicative practice, social sharedness, and appropriateness made for alternative, quasi-oppositional ways of speaking "the regime's" language.

Pramoedya Ananta Toer, Indonesia's leading man of letters, described this situation around the same time Ferguson was developing his ideas about diglossia. In his 1963 account of the "prehistory" of Indonesian, he charted the development of two Malays which he termed not "high" and "low," but "school language" and "working language."

> School language [*basa sekolah*] . . . [was] a means of communication between the colonial government and the people . . . useful only for those who were educated to become civil servants . . . fertilizing the seeds of the bureaucrat. . . . Working language [*basa kerdja*] . . . [was a rubric for the Malay which could] be used at any time . . . developing on its own, growing steadily, practical and available whenever needed, spreading more widely and dynamically than school language. (Pramoedya Ananta Toer 1963)

This language emerged spontaneously among colonial subjects in response to their own needs and, indirectly, to imperial forces – urbanization, trade, commercially based print literacy, etc.

Pramoedya recognized that "school language" had power and value, but only for "vertical communication" across lines of hierarchy within colonial institutions and with colonial subjects. He also recognized how this broad institutional sphere had been identified, part-for-whole, with print-based practices of literacy. Beyond this, he pointed out that Malay was being spoken in communities and contexts which the state could marginalize but not erase, where forms and norms of "good" Malay were not really important. A Marxist who knew a dialectic when he saw one, Pramoedya framed this as a complementary, conflictual dynamic which would be resolved through the two languages' synthesis in the nationalist revolution which would be led, in part, by those he called "civil servants," speakers of the imperial regime's own Malay.

Subaltern languages and their elites

"High" Malay could only serve the NEI by being "projected outward," as Cooper (2005:4) puts it, to a scholarized segment of colonial society. At the same time Malay marked their interstitial position between other natives and the Dutch, members of this group developed into the subaltern elite which could pirate that language for projects of proto-national identity building and anti-colonial resistance.

By the beginning of the 20th century, knowledge of Malay was being "spread" by a network of schools which, like those in the Congo, were established to produce a class of native colonial functionaries. "Highly rationalized, tightly centralized, structurally analogous to the state bureaucracy itself," (Anderson 1991:121) these schools were scattered across the vast expanse of colonial territory, all transmitting the state's unified, print-literate Malay as the key competence for colonial officials.

Viewed from "above," and with an eye to its institutional purpose, this system produced not just High Malay-speaking candidates for government service, but diglossic situations on colonial territory. Viewed from "below," though, and with an eye to the persons who used Malay with each other in those institutions, this system also created groups of natives who shared not only a language but membership in a radically new kind of community.

In *Imagined communities,* Benedict Anderson (1991) describes the coalescence of such groups in the postcolonial dynamic he calls the "last wave of nationalism." He foregrounds imperial Malay's meaningfulness as a commonality among a new group of functionaries whose professions made them migrants, "tender pilgrims" as Anderson calls them, whose careers took them from place to place within the empire. Their paths crossed and ran parallel as each made an "inward, upward" journey through the colonial hierarchy centered on Batavia.

"School Malay" was a constant in these journeys and among those who made them, whose native languages often differed. As part of their shared experience, Anderson suggests, Malay helped them to imagine a society located on the same expanse of territory which they covered in their collective travels, where that language was spoken by more people. Projecting outward and into the future their sense of linguistic sharedness, they helped make Malay focal for the proto-nationalist movement which was formally and publicly declared in 1928 with the slogan "One island, one language, one nationality."

In a way, this appropriation of High Malay mirrors the work by an earlier generation of linguists. They had worked in a text-centered philological mode to describe and partly create literate Malay, and then subaltern elites appropriated print-based "school language" into their lives as a language of experience, one which embodied and helped resolve dilemmas of identity. Perhaps it was the notion that philologists were promoting progress through language which made it easy for the NEI's Dutch rulers to take an easy, custodial attitude to "their" surrogate language of power, not grasping until it was too late that what they had appropriated in one way could be appropriated from them in another.

Why Languages don't Spread

I have sketched Malay's colonial history with an eye to Fabian's description of Swahili, trying to demonstrate the importance of his observation at the head of this chapter. Fabian drew this moral from a project of imperial linguistics in which Belgian functionaries also failed to see that the work of linguists had effects and uses which outran their intentions. This led Fabian to identify social positions and interests which make it convenient and plausible to think of such social and linguistic dynamics as a matter of languages "spreading" across territory. I have touched on Darwinian visions as one element of such views: "stronger," more "progressive" languages "spread" by displacing their less efficient, "weaker" counterparts. Biological metaphors of contagion are plausible partly because they resonate with Herder's organismic vision, be they microbial, as Fabian suggests, or botanical, as in Peter Mühlhaüsler's warnings (1996) about languages which "spread" like weeds, from locale to locale, displacing other languages from their niches.[7]

Jespersen's story of progress in language, together with Gellner's account of national modernity, have helped here to foreground another kind of "language spread." Framing language as a conventional instrument used to talk about the world helps to make language spread a matter of distributing knowledge of those conventions among individuals separated on some expanse of territory. I have suggested, along lines set out by Fabian, that colonialists were able to ignore the fact that the creation of linguistic homogeneity could not be isolated from social dynamics, or linguistic sameness from social sharedness. Perhaps the Belgians, like the Dutch, could not imagine that "their" language (Swahili) could ground oppositional stances and identities, or that it could be anything but "artificial," "secondary," and "safe" just because it had no native speakers or place.[8]

The dynamics I have sketched here have carried over into the postcolonial era, as languages of wider communication are "spreading" at an accelerated rate. Schleicher, Jespersen, and some of their modern day successors would see this as the ongoing victory of stronger languages over weaker. But present-day linguists now regard these developments as pressing intellectual challenges and social problems, whether or not they recognize them as legacies of the colonial era. So in the last chapter I turn to the implications of that past for a science of language which is increasingly obliged to engage not just with languages, but speakers and communities, in a globalizing world.

Notes to chapter 6

1   Relations between ideology and colonial practice were in fact more complex, as Alice Conklin (1997) shows in her discussion of France's West African empire.
2   This debate about language *policy* involved no dispute about language *value*; it was commonly known among all involved that even if a "native" language were "elevated" to the status of a colonial administrative language, it would never for that reason, or in that use, be comparable with English. This shared understanding grounded a debate on policy on the shared awareness of British superiority and imperial legitimacy (see Pennycook 1998, Powell 2002).
3   For an overview of general attitudes to the primitive among Jespersen's colleagues in the field of ethnology, see Henson 1974.
4   For reasons of brevity I do not discuss here the ways Fabian's two-sided approach to this body of work can be applied to the work of colonial linguistics of Swahili in neighboring British Kenya and German (later British) Tanganyika (now Tanzania).
5   But not, it should be noted, "aboriginal" speakers of the unrelated Senoic languages living in remote areas of the peninsula's highlands.

6 For further discussion see Errington 1985, 1988, and sources discussed there.

7 Another metaphor which is less useful here, at least, is developed by Jean-Louis Calvet (1974) in his digestive description of "spread" of languages in sub-Saharan languages as a process of "*glottophagie*," in which they "consume" others.

8 This enduring sense of languages having locales can be read from a silence or gap in the work of colonial linguistics I have not discussed here: a broad disregard for languages which colonial contexts engendered, and which had no "places" of their own. These are so-called creole or "pidgin" languages like that which Fanon made the object of his protest cited in chapter 5. The longstanding marginality of these languages in linguistics has been subject to an extended intellectual, ideological, and theoretical critique by Michel Degraff as "the fallacy of creole exceptionalism; . . . a set of beliefs, widespread among both linguists and nonlinguists, that Creole languages form an exceptional class on phylogenetic and/or typological grounds . . . with nonlinguistic implications" (Degraff 2005:533).

Chapter 7

Postcolonial Postscript

Do we need foreign linguists? Unfortunately, yes.
Demetrio Cojtí, at the 1989 Maya Linguistics Workshop
(quoted in England 1995:140)

But as we mock these genteel fumblers of a previous era, we should prepare ourselves for the jeers of a later century. How come we never think of that? We believe in evolution at least in the sense of evolution culminating in us. We forget that this entails evolution beyond our solipsistic selves.
Julian Barnes, *The lemon table* (2004:105)

Contemporary linguists deal with data and models very different from those I have discussed here. Their field's central agenda, centered on neurocognitive reality, is to deduce a small number of abstract parameters, or "atoms of language" (Baker 2001). By explaining how these parameters combine according to the "mind's hidden rules of grammar," they aim to explain also what count as superficial phenomena of linguistic diversity. New strategies for discovering these universal parameters make an ocean of descriptive details of difference less interesting, and the work of engaging diversity in "the field" a peripheral activity which one committed fieldworker calls, tongue in cheek, "butterfly collecting" (Everett 2004:141).

But the "withering of fieldwork" among academic linguists over the last part of the 20th century has not ended traditions of

linguistic work I have discussed in this book. In this chapter I consider two contemporary engagements with linguistic and human
difference – one obviously rooted in the colonial past, the other less
so – which are reshaping older interests and values, and which
require revised practices and different habits of thought. The main
question here is whether and how such projects differ from those
of an earlier era, and whether linguists are justified in regarding
their field as having left its colonial roots far behind.

I discuss first linguists who have carried over from the colonial
past the double work of conversion sketched in chapters 2 and 5:
missionaries still seeking to transform speakers of exotic languages
in the formerly colonialized world into literate Christians. Once
again I frame a few thin historical slices of this work against a
broader historical and political backdrop. They can be made to
reflect more broadly on the Summer Institute of Linguistics (SIL),
an American organization which now supports missionary linguists
with new methods, goals, and statuses.

My sketch of the SIL's presence in Guatemala is meant to foreground new versions of ambivalences which have always emerged
in the language-centered work of faith, but which seem clearest
when they are articulated by literate native speakers like Demetrio
Cojtí, "dean of Maya public intellectuals" (Warren 1998:74), quoted
above. He speaks of a "field of operation" where missionary linguists have been joined by their secular counterparts, and about a
politics of identity emerging from the contested senses of "ownership" of language which linguists help to create and shape.

This chapter's second main topic is a global trend which now has
a claim on the attention of all linguists: social transformations which
are causing thousands of languages to "die" or at least become
"endangered." The intellectual and political significances of this
impending loss are now redefining linguists' goals, and the strategies they use to describe languages. A glance at the practices of
literacy linguists are introducing in order to "save languages" shows
also the transformative effects their work can have in what Talal
Asad described in 1986 as "monolithic, ineluctable, and titanic
struggle[s] between strong and weak languages." Viewed against
the backdrop of translocal, integrative dynamics of "globalization,"
linguists can be seen as engaged not just in such "local struggles"
but with the larger trajectories of change reviewed in previous

chapters. Now those trajectories are making linguistic diversity into a scarce resource, and so giving linguists reasons to rethink their field's "evolution" in a fast changing world.

Linguistics in a Postcolonial World

The word "postcolonial" has multiple senses because, as a negative label, it identifies things in relation to an era which is no more; so the meanings it can express in a phrase like "postcolonial linguistics" vary as do the enterprises I have sketched in this book. One such postcolonial linguistics is ongoing in nation-states that have inherited colonial borders and infrastructures, where linguistically diverse citizenries recognize the enduring importance of European languages of wider communication. That these are colonial legacies can only partly be disguised by designations like "official language," language of state," and so on. Such labels mute but do not erase durable hierarchies and relations of dependency they help to reproduce, especially between new national elites who control those European languages of power, and others whose competences are restricted to "national," "regional," "ethnic," "tribal" languages, and so on.

According to the logic of "progress in language" outlined in chapter 6, these postcolonial confusions of tongues are both causes and consequences of the backwardness of these "developing" nation-states. A broadly evolutionistic point of view still allows such diversity to be regarded as a barrier to efficient communication which can be overcome by state-centered "language engineering," projects which can answer to Raison-Jourde's description of "scholarization" in 19th century Madagascar, or Ernest Gellner's description of the "exoeducation" and "exosocialization" of citizens of modern nation-states. Where such transformative efforts fail, people of the developing world would seem to rely on European languages as "perpetual consumers of modernity. Europe and the Americas, the only true subjects of history, have thought out on our behalf not only the script of colonial enlightenment and exploitation, but also that of our anticolonial resistance and postcolonial misery" (Chatterjee 1993:5).

Chatterjee's much broader, ironic story of modernity helps here to consider how a "postcolonial linguistics" might figure in the shaping of postcolonial national ideologies, and whether it might have a place in forming new linguistic identities like those discussed in chapters 5 and 6. I suggested there that linguists devised print-literate representations of spoken language by projecting their own social imaginary of national identity and territory, imposing it from above, through language, along with colonial hierarchies. The results of that work are still evident in the ethnopolitics of some developing nations, even if they have become attenuated in others.[1]

Part of Chatterjee's argument about the specter of postcolonial nationalism is, in fact, that some "ethnic languages" had already emerged as languages of modern nationalisms during the colonial era, and as more than lesser likenesses of their European and North American counterparts. By suggesting that British linguists inadvertently produced resources for ethnically based anticolonial resistance in Bengal, he suggests also the possibility of similar projects in other postcolonial nations.[2] He argues that "the Bengali language" could be appropriated by a native, literate, bilingual elite after British linguists developed the orthographic substrate for its print-literate forms. As these developed and circulated, educated Bengalis came to invest "their" language with senses of sharedness and community "outside the purview of the state and the European missionaries" (Chatterjee 1993:7). This became the linguistic ground for a new social formation and an "inner domain of cultural identity, from which the colonial intruder had to be kept out; language therefore became a zone over which the nation first had to declare its sovereignty and then had to transform in order to make it adequate for the modern world" (Chatterjee 1993:7).

Chatterjee's account begins where the work of colonial linguists ended, but is suggestive here for considering unintended uses and effects of work by other linguists on other "ethnic" languages. Where social hierarchies continue to be reproduced in conditions of language difference, he suggests, the results of the work of linguistics might play into analogous projects of autonomy. With this colonial era scenario in mind, I turn to work on the language of people who confront a postcolonial regime grounded in an ethnopolitical hierarchy established by its colonial predecessor.

The New Missionary Linguistics

Most missionaries these days speak English, and most with an American accent. The American Baptist International Mission Board, for instance, currently oversees 5,000 missionaries worldwide, operates with a 282 million dollar budget, and claims a church membership abroad of 7.4 million. Of more interest here, though, is the Summer Institute of Linguistics (SIL). Based at the University of Texas at Arlington, the SIL has trained and supported 5,300 missionary linguists in the study of some 1,000 languages around the world. It is also responsible for coordinating and organizing the single largest, most widely cited compendium of knowledge of global linguistic diversity: *Ethnologue*, produced in print form (Grimes 1984) and also available at www. ethnologue.com.

The SIL's self-described mission is "facilitating language-based development . . . [among] the peoples of the world through research, translation, and literacy" (www.sil.org, accessed February 6, 2007). This public statement passes over the spiritual mission the SIL has taken over from its Protestant colonial forebears, described in chapter 5: the SIL aims to foster literacy as a way of bringing Christianity's transformative power to people as they read the gospel in their native tongues.

This duality of mission suits the postcolonial conditions in which the SIL works, which require that two separate constituencies be addressed. Like other missionary societies before it, the SIL depends for financial support on believers "at home," to whom an "evangelical mission" can be presented independently of the "strange procedure" (Stoll 1982:4) of technical linguistic description. Unlike colonial era organizations, though, the SIL needs support (or at least tolerance) from officials and apparatuses of postcolonial states which govern the people they seek to convert. To this constituency the SIL can present itself as an agency of civilization, working to give literacy to backward peoples in support of "developing" nation-states' own modernizing agendas. This basic duality, and the conflicts it can create, can be sketched along with the history of SIL work among speakers of Mayan languages in the highlands of Guatemala.

The founder of the SIL, Cameron Townsend (1896–1982), had his formative experiences as a young evangelical in Guatemala in the 1920s proselytizing and selling Spanish-language Bibles. Guatemala had by then been independent from Spain for a century, but a series of dictatorships, coups, and stretches of military rule had done little to elevate the status of the Mayan Indians whom Townsend aimed to convert. Then, as now, Mayans comprised a majority of the country's population – currently 5.4 million, or 60 percent – but were politically and economically marginalized by a dominant, Catholic, Spanish-speaking population.

Successors to the Spanish rulers understood that they were also assuming the role of civilizers of the Mayans, as mandated by law in 1824: the Mayan languages were to be rendered extinct because they were "imperfect" and "insufficient for enlightening the people or perfecting their civilization" (quoted in Richards 1989:97). But Townsend heard a different calling in Guatemala's highlands.

According to the SIL's own history (Wallis and Bennett 1959:viii), he began to study the local language, Kaqchikel, after hearing a Mayan's "plaintive plea:" "Why hasn't God learned our language?" By 1931 he had responded with a grammar of Kaqchikel, and a translation of the New Testament. But instead of presenting the first copy of his new translation to this or any other speaker of Kaqchikel, Townsend gave it to the Guatemala's strong man of the moment, Jorge Ubico. Ubico already knew that he and other wealthy Guatemalan landowners had "overlooked a gold mine" (Stoll 1982:42) in the potential pool of Mayan plantation labor, and saw Townsend's linguistic work as a means to that end. Literacy in Mayan languages, Townsend explained, was just the first step towards "Indians acquir[ing] the more prestigious, advantageous [Spanish] tongue, whereupon parents would raise their children as Spanish speakers" (quoted in Stoll 1982:37).

From the outset, then, Townsend foregrounded the civilizing effects and social uses of his linguistic work, in effect promoting "progress through language" by working to induct literate Mayans into the Spanish language, the dominant society, and a national political economy, albeit as subordinated workers on land expropriated from their ancestors. Ubico for his part invited Townsend to continue his work with the neighboring Q'eqchi' Mayans, who were creating trouble on plantations recently established on lands where they had lived.

But Townsend's wider ambitions led him back to the United States in order to train Christian soldiers in techniques of linguistic description who would continue the work of conversion in what was still a colonial world. With a close eye on developments in the American academy, he devised training methods by drawing on "descriptive" or "structural" linguistics, a new discipline whose development marked a sea shift away from comparative philology.

To sketch the break between structural linguistics and comparative philology, it is useful to mention influential arguments made by Ferdinand de Saussure, an eminent Swiss comparative philologist, in lectures he gave just before World War I. While Otto Jespersen was elaborating images of language evolution I sketched in chapter 5, Saussure argued against what he viewed as "absurd notions, prejudices, mirages, and fictions [which] have sprung up" (1966:7) in the older field of philology. Point for point, Saussure denied comparative philologists' claims and assumptions about linguistic change, granting them interest at most from what he called a "psychological viewpoint."[3]

Saussure argued that elements of language are not organically bound to meanings, uses, or users, but are rather entirely conventional, abstract, and virtual. They are not natural organisms but conventional symbols. He regarded speech as a source of data about the recurring patterns which define a language's properties, along lines I set out in chapter 1. In this way Saussure located linguists' objects of descriptions not in territories, or history, but in human minds as sociopsychological (or cognitive, as one might say now) entities. When languages are framed as self-contained systems which are not bound up with any evolutionary force, then change in language counts as the effect of socially disruptive forces which throw those systems into disequilibrium.

Saussure's groundbreaking ideas resonated with approaches to the study of North American languages which were emerging in the United States about the same time. Thanks to a range of developments over the next 30 years, on both sides of the Atlantic, linguists began what one envious anthropologist called their migration across "the border between the social sciences" and the "exact and natural sciences" (Levi-Strauss 1967:68).

Townsend adapted these new approaches and ideas to train missionaries at what he called Camp Wycliffe, and later renamed the SIL. He saw in this new science the prospect that a set of rigorous procedures, properly learned and applied, could allow any missionary to reduce any language to writing. (This was the dream of what professional linguists came to call, tongue in cheek, "cookbook linguistics.") Townsend was in contact, for instance, with Edward Sapir, a major figure among the new linguists whose insights into the "psychological reality" of sound types, or phonemes,[4] he incorporated into his own "psychophonemic" methods for reducing speech to writing. Though he declined Sapir's invitation to study with him at Yale, one of his own protégés, Kenneth Pike, began a career there which was illustrious not just because he assumed the presidency of the SIL from 1942 to 1979, but because of academic publications like *Phonemics: a technique for reducing languages to writing* (Pike 1947).[5]

The new linguistics was also rhetorically useful, because it allowed Townsend to claim the mantle of scientist, and ideologically useful because it provided a guide for developing intimate yet asymmetrical relations with native speakers of the languages missionaries sought to describe. For them, natives counted as sources of the data which, under analysis, let them understand a language better than its speakers. By analyzing an abstract, underlying system, linguists were able to establish their own more profound understanding of how "sounds [of a language] are automatically and unconsciously organized by the native into structural units . . . [in] varieties a trained foreigner might detect but which a native speaker may be unaware of" (Pike 1947:57).

So, too, scientific neutrality and objectivity made linguists not just exponents of civilization and reason, but the bringers of "descriptive linguistics to country after country for the announced purpose of foreign national unity" (Stoll 1982:63). These dual purposes were given sharper institutional shape in 1942, when Townsend created another organization, the Wycliffe Bible Translators (WBT), which operated much in the manner of missionary organizations discussed in chapter 5 to support the publishing of

Christian texts in languages that SIL workers studied. The WBT and SIL shared a board of directors, but the semblance of an institutional division of labor lent plausibility to both kinds of work, and reflected more clearly the double task of describing languages before using them to translate holy writ. This linking of intellectual and textual traditions gave rise to a "spectacle of dedication [faith] and technology [science] which invites endless speculation" (Stoll 1982:6) about missionaries' purposes and motives.

A Newer Linguistics and a Newer Politics

During the Cold War, SIL linguists were able to gain long-term access to regions and communities of the postcolonial world which were off limits to other Americans and Europeans. Across much of what came to be called the Third World, the SIL enlarged its fields of operation, often in parallel with expanding American military, political, and economic interests. Ample evidence of SIL workers' complicity with these larger agendas of power and capital, especially in the New World, has been gathered by David Stoll in *Fishers of men or founders of empire?* (1982) and Gerard Colby and Charlotte Dennett in their aptly titled *Thy will be done* (1995). Of interest here, though, are more local, ambiguous dimensions of what always and everywhere justified the SIL's presence: the work of reducing speech to writing.

Townsend dispatched some of his students to study Mayan languages in Guatemala, where they were supported by an agency established in Guatemala's Ministry of Education: the Instituto Indigenista Nacional (IIN), which promoted "literacy [in Spanish] and castillianization" (López 1989:31 quoted in French 2003:488). Together, the IIN and SIL convened the First Linguistic Conference (Primer Congreso de Lingüistica) in 1949 to coordinate their strategies for dealing with another instance of the challenge I discussed in chapter 4: different linguists in different regions, working on different languages, were unfortunately producing "multiple forms of graphic representation for the indigenous languages of the country" (IIN 1950:5 quoted in French 2003:488).

In fact the SIL and IIN aimed to devise one orthography which could serve two incompatible goals. On one side were the metrics of empirical accuracy; on the other, the demands of "progress" for uniform ways of writing diverse Mayan languages, so that speakers could be quickly assimilated to the Spanish-speaking, Guatemalan citizenry. The second of these criteria carried the day. Following Townsend's strategy, conference participants devised a unified orthography for Mayan languages in the image of Spanish spelling. So, for instance, the single digraph *qu* was chosen as a symbol for a range of significantly different speech sounds in various Mayan languages, some only vaguely resembling the sound it represents in Spanish writing. So the name of one Mayan language was spelled Quiché, even though that word's first sound has a pronunciation and sound qualities quite distinct from that which *qu* represents in Spanish.[6]

The conference's agenda was complicated also by a small but troublesome constituency of newly literate Mayans, educated largely by the SIL, who by 1945 had begun to devise their own orthographies of their languages. In this way they not only sought more accurate orthographies for their peoples' speech, but practices of literacy which could mark an "inner domain of cultural identity," as Chatterjee calls it. By rejecting Spanish images for Mayan speech they rejected, part-for-whole, the assimilationist policies the SIL and IIN so transparently supported.

Struggle ensued between "strong" and "weak" languages as these Mayans tried to develop infrastructures of literacy which mirrored and opposed those of dominant outsiders. In the early 1940s, an association of Mayan teachers and an Academy of Mayan languages were founded, one of their members also the designer of a new orthography. Adrián Chavéz could claim for it not just authenticity but superior accuracy: he devised symbols for distinct sounds which SIL linguists had either failed to recognize, or elected to ignore as too inconveniently different from Spanish. So, for instance, Chavéz used *k'*, not *qu*, to represent the first sound in the name of his native language, K'iche', and further differentiated Mayan from Spanish writing by adapting characters from precolonial Mayan systems of writing. These had been largely destroyed by the Conquistadores as the work of the devil, but counted for him as "genuinely indigenous symbols" which represented "the marvelous beauty of the old culture" (quoted in French 2003:487).

Chavéz's orthography may have been more accurate than the SIL's, but without a political and institutional infrastructure it could not "spread" to members of other communities of speakers of different Mayan languages. This situation began to change, though, in the 1970s, along with the local ethnopolitics of language, and guiding ideas of academic linguistics. This second development came to Guatemala with secular linguists guided not by religious calling but by a "political subjectivity" (Warren 1998:x): witnesses to the civil rights and antiwar movement in the United States and a brutal counterinsurgency movement being waged by the government against Mayans.

In 1971 a new nongovernmental organization (NGO) was founded as a venue for linguistic projects which were both intellectually and politically motivated. The Proyecto Lingüistico Francisco Marroquín (PLFM) – begun by a Briton and a few Americans, one a research linguist – offered to train Mayans in the field to a level of proficiency comparable with that of a Master's degree. But by this time a paradigm shift in American linguistics had given rise to new research strategies.

In the 1960s Noam Chomsky reframed the conundrum of linguistic unity and diversity by focusing on the genetic capacities of every human to learn any language. He posed a simple, compelling question: how is it that any normal human child is able to learn a language – that is, becomes capable of producing and understanding indefinitely large numbers of sentences in that language – after comparatively limited, fragmentary exposure to its use? This question shifted the field's explanatory focus to the study of grammatical phenomena for clues to the nature of a species-wide language faculty, manifested in each individual's linguistic competence.

Framed in this way, linguistic research requires as data not just instances of native speech, but intuitions native speakers have about speech, based on internalized knowledge which allows them to distinguish just those combinations of words which count as "acceptable" or "well formed" in their language. For the study of English, for instance, it became significant that speakers recognize that "It is easy to please John" is acceptable, but "It is eager to please John" is not. This is evidence of underlying "rules" of English which speakers internalize as part of their competence.

Because "acceptability judgments" must be elicited, and not just observed, linguists needed new techniques and ways of engaging speakers, posing questions which only native speakers could answer. They were no longer Pike's unknowing producers of data, but possessors of knowledge which made them privileged interlocutors. In principle, at least, the best analysis can be done by a native speaker, which is one reason linguists in North America and European increasingly turned to the study of their own languages, contributing to what Everett called the "withering of field work."

Chomsky's new paradigm, and new ways of engaging speakers in "the field," made it increasingly advantageous for linguists to engage closely and collegially with speakers of Mayan languages, and by 1976 the PLFM was fully in the hands of Mayan "native speakers/analysts," who brought together "expert knowledge, scientific analysis, and Maya professionalization" (French 2003:493). Working in the tradition of Adrián Chavéz, they began describing Mayan languages with scientific techniques, and for an inner domain of Mayan cultural identity, doing genuine and rich postcolonial linguistics. As lines blurred between linguist and native speaker, literate and illiterate, "civilized" and "uncivilized," Mayans were able to criticize work by SIL linguists on both social and empirical grounds, pointing to inconsistencies and empirical gaps which threw their privileged status as scientists into doubt. Already by 1977, SIL workers were shifting alignments away from the metrics of science to the values of progress, arguing that the paramount need was for literacy among "ethnic minorities" who were to eventually become Spanish speakers.

Only from this point of view could the SIL criticize Mayans' linguistic work, not as inaccurate but impractical, threatening to "hinder their own people in making appropriate gains in the mestizo world" (Henne 1991:5). This criticism effectively presupposed a class hierarchy within Mayan communities corresponding to that which had existed previously between Mayans and "outsiders" who had dealings with them. These native linguists counted as "elites," as Henne put it, who had usurped the SIL's place to pit their own agenda against one which was ostensibly more acceptable among less educated but more practically oriented Mayan "educators" whom the SIL counted as partners and allies.

With new ethnic violence perpetrated by the Guatemalan state on Mayans in the 1980s, the PLFM's work took on new urgency in a language-centered politics of recognition and a project of linguistic self-determination. Its goal was recognition not just for the authenticity of all Mayan identities, but also their internally plural ethnolinguistic character, described in the charter of another NGO of native linguists as grounding "[t]he Mayan nation['s] . . . own values that constitute a great human richness. Among those strongest values that are found are the twenty Mayan languages spoken today" (Oxlajuuj Keej Maya' Ajtz'iib quoted in translation in French 2003:495).

As part of a postcolonial, liberationist dynamic, the nativist linguistic project can be seen as enlisting practices of literacy in struggles between "weak" languages and a "strong" one. But those practices could not be adapted without politically and culturally difficult effects, sketched in previous chapters: even when they focused on particular languages, native linguists had to devise strategies of selection to resolve differences and create gaps between unitary letters and diversities of speech. Part of the conflictedness Cojtí expressed in this chapter's first epigraph can be traced to this dimension of Mayans' literacy-centered engagements with their own languages.

Cojtí made this remark with an eye to enduring inequalities and difference in interests between speakers of Mayan languages on one hand, and foreign academics on the other. He insisted that foreign scientists had no license to avoid politics in their particular zones of postcolonial contact:

> It is difficult, above all in Guatemala, where Ladino colonialism reigns . . . for linguists to define themselves as neutral or apolitical, since they work on languages that are sentenced to death and officially demoted. In this country, the linguist who works on Mayan languages only has two options: either active complicity in the prevailing colonialism and linguistic assimilationism, or activism in favor of a new linguistic order in which equality in the rights of all language is made concrete. (Cojtí 1990:19 quoted in translation in England 1995:139)

Even foreign linguists who recognize these obligations cannot shed their roles as "[o]utsiders . . . [who are] both resented and viewed as useful sources of information" (England 1995:141).

But native linguists can also have trouble finding middle ground among fellow speakers of languages outside their own expert circles. They are not always immune from suspicion that they are prescribing rather than describing a language, and an identity which goes with it. Nikte' Sis Iboy, for instance, is a linguist who studied her native Achi language and described it on structural grounds as a dialect of K'iche', the larger Mayan language mentioned above. This earned her accusations from some other Achi speakers that she was trying (like SIL linguists before her) to "destroy their [Achi] identity" (England 2003:739). Any response based simply on "facts" about these languages would fail to engage that criticism in its own terms, leaving her, like other linguists in other situations, unable to control the meanings and uses of her work.

Indigenist Identities and Languages

These politics of linguistics emerge when linguists seek to help speakers remake their "weak" languages in the literate image of encroaching "strong" ones. But they can only produce relatively simple images of linguistic complexity which circulate not just as descriptions, but templates for practices of literacy with meanings and uses which can shift among speakers and contexts.

What Cojtí described as the "death sentence" placed on Mayan languages is a dramatic instance of larger patterns of social and linguistic change around the world. Though they may not be threatened by an oppressive state, other communities and their languages are being affected by flows of people, capital, and information which commonly go by the name "globalization." Some see this as just the newest phase of the integrative dynamic I have traced in the work of colonial linguists, which will continue to homogenize the world's peoples and the ways they speak. Others see instead a "massive human-made extinction crisis of languages and cultures" (www.terralingua.org, accessed 6/9/06).

In *The origins of Indigenism: human rights and the politics of identity*, Ronald Niezen (2003) foregrounds a paradox of globalization: the same forces which threaten marginal communities and languages are also creating communication channels, contexts, and global audiences which members of those communities can use to claim rights to local autonomy. When members of otherwise scattered communities recognize their common predicament, they can devise common responses to similar encroaching forces (political, economic, and environmental). Over the last 20 years, transnational forums have developed where indigenous peoples from different conditions have been able to "defiantly enter the public sphere" and where "leaders from Asian, northern Europe, Africa, the Americas, and the South Pacific . . . meet . . . to discuss the development of human rights standards for indigenous peoples" (Niezen 2003: 3–4).

Claims for local autonomy need to be issued to global audiences with vocabularies and rhetorics which all parties can understand, if not always in the same ways. So in these contexts, issues of "language" have been invoked with different accents by different speakers, for different audiences. The organistic tradition of thought about language I discussed in chapters 3 and 4 is still a strong and well-traveled means for associating language with place, identity, and history, and for asserting rights to territories through language and "natural" genealogical links between speakers and their distant ancestral pasts. These have the potential to trump historically "shallower" claims of "outsiders" and "newcomers," and so to contribute to what Amy Muehlebach (2001) calls "place-making strategies" of indigenous peoples.

Images of such organic links between people and environments via language are being mobilized in support of many claims to indigenous rights. In venues like the Indigenous Peoples' and Globalization seminar of July 2001, for instance, the Anishinaabe activist Winona Laduke from Minnesota said:

> [the] teachings of our people concerning our relationships to the land are deeply embedded in our language. . . . Without our languages, we are simply wandering – philosophically, spiritually, economically. To preserve our languages we need to protect our lands and our historic practices. (Mander and Tauli-Corpuz n.d.:19)

Jeanette Armstrong, of the Okanagans of British Columbia, echoed Laduke at that meeting by offering a single definition of the Okanagan words meaning "our place on the land" and "our language:" "We think of our language as the language of the land. This means

that the land has taught us our language" (Mander and Tauli-
Corpuz n.d.:31).[7]

The broader cultural grounds for understanding meaningful, real
linkages between languages and locales can differ, and do not necessarily translate as easily as statements which affirm that they
exist. But this need not detract from their rhetorical effectiveness if
they resonate with other understandings of languages as ways of
"being-in-the-world" (Muehlebach 2001:416). Claims to local rights
and languages have to fit such understandings if they are to circulate in translocal networks. Certainly the new rhetorics of local
identity would be recognizable to Herder, as would descriptions of
indigenist struggles as parts of a battle against the "third extinction
crisis" (Maffi 1999:21) which, after loss of biodiversity and traditional cultures, extends to language.

At a 1992 UN Conference on Environment and Development
vocabularies of indigenous languages figured centrally in discussion of them as "repositories of vast accumulations of traditional
knowledge and experience" (Brundtland 1987:114). Only with a
sense of language-in-the-world like that I have discussed here – its
situatedness in natural environments, the purity of its origins, and
so on – is it intuitively plausible that the "death" of a language
marks an "extinction of experience" (Nabhan and St. Antoine 1993).
Now this old vision of language has new implications for linguistics. It promotes an indigenist linguistics centered not just on the
work of reducing of speech to writing, or contributing to the archive
of linguistic knowledge, but also and most crucially nurturing a
language in its native habitat:

> [T]here is a very close parallel between [*ex situ*] language preserva-
> tion and ex situ conservation in biology: while both serve an impor-
> tant function, in both cases the ecological context is ignored. Just as
> seed banks cannot preserve a plant's biological ecology, ex situ
> linguistic documentation can not preserve a language's linguistic
> ecology. (Skutnabb-Kangas 1999:46)

But unlike the work of linguists discussed in chapters 5 and 6, who
understood that they were engaged with impure remnants of "pure"
original languages, these situations require that the present (or near
past) be taken as a point of purity which needs to be guarded

against the hybridizing effects of future contact with "outside" languages. Images of linguistic and cultural purity can themselves have different uses and effects in different contexts, as is demonstrated by Renée Sylvain's review of claims to indigenous sovereignty made on behalf of the San people of South Africa: "[t]he more essentialized the 'cultural' [and linguistic] features become, the more they are seen as contrary to the historically transitory features of political economy" (Sylvain 2002:1076).

Linguists working in these postcolonial "zones of contact" now find that they need to gauge the collateral effects of their work in fine-grained ways: what "borrowed" words, grammatical constructions, or idioms, for instance, should find a place in their descriptions? What in an orthography they devise might help, hinder, or skew "indigenous" literacies in different varieties of a language, sustaining some better than others in ongoing struggles with "strong" languages? The social importance of such narrow, empirical questions might be much clearer in the postcolonial than the colonial era, now that linguists recognize that they do their work in zones of contact populated by multiple voices and interests, and are not just describing speech but promoting practices of literacy.

Unintended Consequences

Linguists share no party line or agenda for dealing with language death and endangerment. The late and distinguished Peter Ladefoged, among the field's foremost connoisseurs of linguistic diversity, went on record in 1992 with a call to his colleagues to recognize that speakers of "endangered languages" can decide, in their own lives and on their own terms, which of several languages is best for them and their children. On the other hand Steven Pinker, well-known social Darwinist and sociobiologist, asserts that "[e]very time a language dies, we lose thousands of unique insights, metaphors, and other acts of genius" (Endangered Language Fund n.d.). Here he draws on ideas and sentiments from the relativist tradition of linguistics which I have sketched in this book, and which he has stridently attacked in his own work (Pinker 1995).[8]

Linguists can motivate their studies of endangered languages locally or globally. Local views are bound up with the romanticist past, privileging uniqueness as intrinsically valuable. Global views, on the other hand, recognize the value of any one language's location in the full spectrum of human linguistic diversity, and as a potential source of evidence for the discovery of universal attributes of language. This position can be framed with Mark Baker's metaphor of the "atoms of language," noted above. Just as Mendeleev could only conceive of the periodic table after isolating and comparing properties of many different kinds of elements, so too linguists can only hope to grasp underlying principles or parameters of language by isolating and comparing properties of many different kinds of languages. If languages "die out" before they have been studied, linguists can not be confident that they have fully grasped their underlying unity.[9]

From this latter position, languages have a different status as facts, or "data." It brings with it more concern for sufficiently complete records of phenomena of speech than the prospect that the language in question will "die" in the future. But this dispassionately framed position has its own political implications for zones of postcolonial contact between linguists and speakers. As Steven Pinker's comment quoted above illustrates, this global view promotes what Jane Hill (2002) has called the "hyperbolic valorization" of languages as having value transcending any speaker or community of speakers. When languages count as part of the universal "property" of mankind, it is "we" (not they) who lose, as Pinker puts it, if one dies. This is, in effect, a claim to languages that some speakers refuse to accept, as in the Hopi and Cupeño communities of the southwest United States which Hill describes.

So challenges and conundrums confront those who continue the work of linguistics in a postcolonial world. A linguist may not recognize speakers' rights of "ownership" of languages he or she seeks to describe, but must recognize that he or she cannot "own" that work. One last example is worth using to show how the lesson of unintended consequences was learned by linguists working to "save" an endangered language in the 1970s, well before globalization's effects on linguistic diversity became a widely discussed issue.

Kenneth Rehg, a student of Micronesian languages, spoken on tiny islands flung across the face of the western Pacific ocean, has recently described his work with colleagues at the University of Hawai'i when they saw that a foreign presence (mostly American) was affecting the ways the local languages were spoken; English was "spreading" among their native speakers. Recognizing the "threat" posed to these languages, they assumed ("perhaps arrogantly" as one put it) that they had "not only a role, but a responsibility to help preserve" them (Topping 2003:524 quoted in Rehg 2004:498).

Driven by what Topping later called a "messianic complex," these linguists initiated the Pacific Languages Development Project (PLDP) which eventually resulted in the writing of grammars of seven Micronesian languages, and dictionaries of five. These were first steps in the project's efforts to teach literacy in these languages in the islands' schools. I focus here on the language of Pohnpeian, spoken on Pohnpei, a roughly circular island just 13 miles across which is now home to about 30,000 people, roughly one-fourth of them foreigners. Pohnpeian is interesting because it presented these linguists with the fewest "dialect problems," and already had what was "probably the closest to . . . a widely accepted standard spelling system" (Rehg 2004:509).

There was only one "dialect problem," really an accentual difference in the pronunciation of a few vowels. Speakers of Pohnpeian's northern dialect pronounced some words with a vowel ɛ (as in "pet"), which speakers of the southern (or Kitti) dialect pronounced with the vowel ɔ (as in "caught").[10] So the Pohnpeian word which can be translated as "spouse" is pronounced in the north as *wɛrɛk*, and in the south as *wɔrɔk*. But some words are pronounced identically in the two dialects, using the ɛ vowel (for instance, the word which means "run aground", *sɛr*).

Twenty years previously, the linguist Paul Garvin devised what he called a "cross-dialect grapheme" to capture this correspondence. He made one symbol stand for both pronunciations, a solution which he reported was "enthusiastically received by both [southern] and [northern] dialect speakers, as the only way in which acceptance by both dialect communities could be assured" (Garvin 1954:121 quoted in Rehg 2004:508). Twenty years later, though, linguists who were seeking to introduce different practices of literacy found that Garvin's orthography was inadequate, but were hard put to devise a better solution.

Garvin saw that when a speaker of Pohnpeian was reading, they would "naturally" pronounce the "cross-dialect grapheme" in accordance with their dialect, northern (as ε) or southern (as $\mathrm{ɔ}$). But when speakers set out to write Pohnpeian, they could not be sure whether they should write a given word with the "cross-dialect" symbol or not, since a speaker of the northern dialect could not know (unless familiar with the southern dialect) whether it was pronounced with the ε vowel or not. To resolve this problem, the PLDP convened a committee which decided to use a symbol corresponding to the northern accent. (There were more northern dialect speakers on the PLDP committee, and their southern-speaking counterparts acceded to their wish.)

What might seem a minor matter of spelling to outsiders turned out to be an issue in southern Pohnpei. Residents there asserted their dialect's difference, and ensured its preservation in writing, by stipulating in the district constitution that local pronunciation be reflected in all official documents (Rehg 2004:509). This counted not just as a collective, official response to an encroaching "outside" power, but a reflex of a more fundamental sense of linguistic identity that Pohnpeians had only partly come to share:

> Before the advent of the new orthography, the [southern] dialect was considered to be of the same status as the Northern dialect. Traditionally, Pohnpeians did not judge people's speech on the basis of where they were from; rather, they evaluated it on the basis of social appropriateness and eloquence. What is at issue here, then, is the common controversy that arises in relation to issues about who owns the language. (Rehg 2004:509)

The work of linguists in postcolonial Pohnpei in this way had "unintended consequences" extending beyond the teaching of letters for speech sounds to the learning of a new sense of ownership. Like their forebears, these linguists brought literacy's indirect but powerful shaping effects to bear on Pohnpei, creating new senses of the value of speech, and of speakers as social beings.

Considering this recent work against a historical backdrop helps to recognize that linguists cannot avoid shaping the zones of postcolonial contact where they engage with endangered languages. It also shows how the work of linguists in a postcolonial world may be scientific, but is never insulated from the worlds of those who speak what they study.

The Truth, and Something Besides the Truth

I have sketched the progress of linguistics in a globalizing world by emphasizing the preoccupations and prejudices of an older, genteel philology which were abandoned as questions about a panhuman "language faculty" have come into ascendance. But I have also argued by example that when linguists enter and create zones of postcolonial contact with speakers of endangered languages, they must navigate newer versions of older conundrums without much guidance from their descriptive metrics. When linguists describe their fields of operation as scenes not just of "contact" but "collision," "competition," or "conflict" (Joseph et al. 2003), they acknowledge that there are issues and requirements in their work which fall beyond the purview of their science.

So the science of language needs to seek purchase on these new yet old challenges which linguists confront "in the field." Otherwise the progressive flattening of linguistic diversity in a globalizing world will make the field's investment in the universal properties of "Language," rather than in individual languages, seem increasingly solipsistic. As both a theoretical and practical matter, linguists are increasingly obliged to think through their work's entanglement with contexts, projects, and ideas from the earlier era.

Perhaps linguists can recognize more fully their work's situated, provisional character. Perhaps essentialized images of languages, either as natural organisms or neurocognitive systems, may serve better when describing a language spoken by people concerned less with its purity than its social meanings and uses. Recognizing difference and conflict within communities can be recognized as a fact of linguistic life as much as social life.

Daniel Everett, an accomplished field linguist who has studied exotic languages spoken along the Amazon river, makes a parallel point by invoking the philosopher William James as a guide for his broadly pragmatic, "coherent" fieldwork. The linguist's obligation, James gives him license to argue, is less to "truth" than coherence, such that "whatever I say . . . about one aspect of my object should cohere with other statements I have made about the object, and the sum of my experience with the object" (Everett 2004:142). This might be a new and not just a different way of developing a more holistic linguistics if, as Everett suggests, it opens up a language's status as an "object" to revision in the course of research, rather than being assumed to dictate its predetermined directions. Coherence depends on engaging dimensions of linguistic experience which may come to be known only through research, which is to say in zones of contact with people who are not just producers of data, but interlocutors.

Such a program would run against the grain of linguistics in the current universalist paradigm, as well as that of linguistics during the colonial era I have discussed in this book. First, it would have to take seriously contrasting and variable modes of speech and expressiveness, just the kinds of complexities which colonial linguists stripped away when they reduced "native" speech to writing, and reduced languages to their own purposes. Second, this work would require linguists to recognize, with Demetrio Cojtí, that power differences are always in the zones of contact which they create in and for their work. These are differences which may be impossible to eradicate but, once recognized, may help to develop broadened agendas and strategies: if those differences become more explicit for all concerned, counting as topics in and not just as enabling conditions for the work of linguistic description, perhaps the field can find a different place in a postcolonial world.

Notes to chapter 7

1 One of the clearest examples of such a situation is South Africa, as the work of colonial linguists survives in the present configuration of "ethnicities." For discussion see de Klerk 2002.
2 This question bears very obviously on the politics of national languages for Swahili in Kenya and Tanzania, and for Indonesian in Indonesia. But the political and cultural pressures mediated by these languages came to the fore as they came into the hands of government officials – technocrats of education – rather than linguists in the narrower sense of the word I have been using here. Discussion of these languages by historians, political scientists, anthropologists, and

others is extensive. Blommaert 1999 provides a good discussion of the complex politics of Swahili in Tanzania; Sneddon's 2003 state-centered history of Indonesian can be read together with more politically oriented reviews by Anderson (1990), Errington (1998), and Vikor (1988).

3   For evidence, however, of the influence of philological cum racialist theories of language history on Saussure's thought, see the discussion of his and his brother's interaction with Adolphe Pictet in articles by John Joseph (2003 and 2000, respectively).

4   Sapir's famous article on this concept is called "The psychological reality of the phoneme" (1949b); his much more general book, *Language* (1949a), covers a wider range of issues and shows more clearly his intellectual debt to the romantic tradition I discussed in earlier chapters.

5   But Townsend's awareness of the embeddedness of language in cultures and contexts is evident from his care to include in his curriculum the study of "customs, psychology, superstitions, vices, economic and cultural status" of peoples to be missionized (Wallis and Bennett 1959:46).

6   In Castilian spelling *qu* represents what linguists call a velar stop, whereas the first sound in the name of this Mayan language, now more commonly written *k'*, is a velar ejective.

7   For a sensitive ethnographic account of another way of linking land and language among a North American people, see Basso 1990.

8   Another linguist who has warned his colleagues against their prejudices in favor of endangered languages is Salikoko Mufwene (2003). His and Ladefoged's considered arguments benefit from comparison with less informed celebrations of language death, some measured, like Malik 2000, and others straightforwardly ethnocentric, like John Miller's (2002) editorial in the *Wall Street Journal*.

9   A newer biological metaphor for this process is developed by a student of aboriginal languages, Robert Dixon, in his book *The rise and fall of languages* (1997), borrowing Stephen Gould's punctuated equilibrium model of speciation. Conversely, ecologists – for example, William Sutherland (2003) – see the problems of endangered languages and species on a global basis as broadly parallel, statistically relatable processes. One need only understand languages to be differentiable members of a species, or species of a genus, instead of part of the fabric of shared experience in communities of speakers.

10   I use symbols of the International Phonetic Alphabet here.

References

Aarsleff, H. 1982. The tradition of Condillac: the problem of the origin of language in the eighteenth century and the debate in the Berlin Academy before Herder. In *From Locke to Saussure: essays on the study of language and intellectual history*. Minneapolis: University of Minnesota Press. 146–209.

Aarsleff, H. 1983. Sir William Jones and the New Philology. In *The study of language in England, 1780–1860*. Minneapolis: University of Minnesota Press. 115–161.

Abrams, P. 1988 [1977]. Notes on the difficult of studying the state. *Journal of historical sociology* 1(1):58–88.

Adam, A. 1995. *The vernacular press and the emergence of the modern Indonesia consciousness (1855–1913)*. Ithaca, NY: Cornell University Press.

Alter, S. G. 1999. *Darwinism and the linguistic image: language, race, and natural theology in the nineteenth century*. Baltimore: Johns Hopkins University Press.

de Alva, K. 1982. Spiritual conflict and accommodation in New Spain: towards a typology of Aztec responses to Christianity. In Collier, G., Rosaldo, R. and Wirth, J. (eds) *The Inca and Aztec states 1400–1800*. New York: Academic Press. 345–366.

Anderson, B. 1990. *Language and power: exploring political cultures in Indonesia*. Ithaca, NY: Cornell University Press.

Anderson, B. 1991. *Imagined communities*, 2nd edn. New York: Verso.

Appadurai, A. 1981. *Worship and conflict under colonial rule: a South Indian case*. New York: Cambridge University Press.

Asad, T. 1986. The concept of cultural translation in British social anthropology. In Clifford, J. and Marcus, G. (eds) *Writing culture: the poetics and politics of ethnography*. Berkeley: University of California Press. 141–164.

Baker, M. 2001. *The atoms of language: the mind's hidden rules of grammar*. New York: Basic Books.

Balibar, R. 1991. The nation form: history and ideology. In Balibar, E. and Wallerstein, I. *Race, nation, class: ambiguous identities*. London: Verso. 86–106.

Barnes, J. 2004. The revival. In Barnes, J. *The lemon table*. Knopf: New York. 97–116.

Basso, K. H. 1990. Speaking with names: language and landscape among the Western Apache. In *Western Apache language and culture – essays in linguistic anthropology*. Tucson: University of Arizona Press. 175–182.

Bauman, R. and Briggs, C. L. 2003. Language, poetry, and Volk in eighteenth-century Germany: Johann Gottfried Herder's construction of tradition. In *Voices of modernity – language ideologies and the politics of inequality*. New York: Cambridge University Press.

Baynham, M. 1995. *Literacy practices: investigating literacy in social contexts*. London: Longman.

Beidelman, T. O. 1982. *Colonial evangelism: a socio-historical study of an East African mission at the grassroots*. Bloomington: Indiana University Press.

Benes, K. 2001. German linguistic nationhood, 1806–1866: philology, cultural translation, and historical identity in preunification Germany. Ph.D. dissertation, University of Washington.

Benes, K. 2004. Comparative linguistics as ethnology: in search of Indo-Germans in Central Asia, 1770–1830. *Comparative Studies of South Asia, Africa, and the Middle East* 24(2):117–132.

Benfey, T. 1869. *Geschichte der sprachwissenschaft und orientalischen philologie in Deutschland*. [History of linguists and oriental philology in Germany.] Munich: Cotta.

Besnier, N. 1995. *Literacy, emotion and authority: reading and writing on a Polynesian atoll*. New York: Cambridge University Press.

Blommaert, J. 1999. *State ideology and language in Tanzania*. Köln: Rüdiger Köppe Verlag.

Blommaert, J. 2005. *From fieldnotes to grammar: artefactual ideologies and the production of languages in Africa*. Universiteit Gent-Vakgroep Afrikaanse Talen en Culturen Research Report No. 6. Gent: Academic Press.

Boone, E. and Mignolo, W. (eds) 1994. *Writing without words: alternative literacies in Mesoamerica and the Andes*. Durham: Duke University Press.

Bopp, F. 1816. *Über das Conjugationssystem der Sanskritsprache in Vergleichung mit jenem der griechischen, lateinischen, persischen und germanischen Sprache*. [On the conjugation system of Sanskrit in comparison with those of Greek, Latin, Persian and German languages.] Frankfurt am Main: Andreïsche Buchhandlung.

Bopp, F. 1827. Review of Grimm 1822–1826. *Jahrbücher für wissenschaftliche Kritik*. Feb:251–256 and May:725–729.

Bourdieu, P. 1977. *Outline of a theory of practice*, trans. R. Nice. New York: Cambridge University Press.

Bourdieu, P. 1993. The field of cultural production. In Johnson, R. (ed.) *The field of cultural production: essays on art and literature*. New York: Columbia University Press. 29–144.

Brundtland, G. 1987. *Our common future*. World commission on environment and development. Oxford: Oxford University Press.

Van Bulck, G. 1948. *Les recherches linguistiques au Congo Belge*. Mémoires de l'Institut Royal Colonial Belge, Section des Sciences Morales et Politiques, vol. 16. Brussels: Imprimeur de l'Académie Royal de Belgique.

Burkhart, L. M. 1989. *The slippery earth: Nahua–Christian moral dialogue in sixteenth century Mexico*. Tempe: University of Arizona Press.

Caldwell, R. 1856. *A comparative grammar of the Dravidian or south-Indian family of languages*. Madras: University of Madras.

Calvet, J.-L. 1974. *Linguistique et colonialisme: petit traité de glottophagie*. Paris: Payot.

Campa, A. 1931. The churchmen and the Indian languages of New Spain. *Hispanic American Historical Review* XI:542–550.

Carochi, H. 2001 [1645]. *Grammar of the Mexican language with an explanation of its adverbs*, trans. J. Lockhart. Stanford: Stanford University Press.

Carrasco, P. 1982. The political economy of the Aztec and Inca states. In Collier, G., Rosaldo, R. and Wirth, J. (eds) *The Inca and Aztec states 1400–1800*. New York: Academic Press. 24–39.

de las Casas, B. 1971. *Bartolomé de las Casas; a selection of his writings*, trans. and ed. G. Sanderlin. New York: Knopf.

de Certeau, M. 1984. *The practice of everyday life*, trans. S. Rendall. Berkeley: University of California Press.

Chatterjee, P. 1993. *The nation and its fragments: colonial and postcolonial histories*. Princeton: Princeton University Press.

Chimhundu, H. 1992. Early missionaries and the ethnolinguistic factor during the "Invention of Tribalism" in Zimbabwe. *Journal of African History* 33:87–109.

Clifford, J. 1982. *Person and myth: Maurice Leenhardt in the Melanesian world*. Berkeley: University of California Press.

Clifford, J. 1992. Traveling cultures. In Grossberg, L., Nelson, C. and Teichler, P. (eds) *Cultural studies*. New York: Routledge. 96–116.

Coe, M. D. and Van Stone, M. 2001. *Reading the Maya Glyphs*. New York: Thames and Hudson.

Cohn, B. 1996a. Introduction. In *Colonialism and its forms of knowledge: the British in India*. Princeton: Princeton University Press. 3–15.

Cohn, B. 1996b. The command of language and the language of command. In *Colonialism and its forms of knowledge: the British in India*. Princeton: Princeton University Press. 16–56.

Colby, G. and Dennett, C. 1995. *Thy will be done – the conquest of the Amazon: Nelson Rockefeller and evangelisms in the age of oil*. New York: Harper Collins.

Collins, J. and Blot, R. 2003. *Literacy and literacies: texts, power, and identity*. New York: Cambridge University Press.

Comaroff, J. and Comaroff, J. 1991. *Of revelation and revolution*. Chicago: University of Chicago Press.

Conklin, A. 1997. A mission to civilize: the Republican idea of empire in France and West Africa, 1895–1930. Stanford: Stanford University Press.

Cooper, F. 2005. *Colonialism in question: theory, knowledge, history*. Berkeley: University of California Press.

Cooper, F. and Stoler, A. (eds) 1997. *Tensions of empire: colonial cultures in a bourgeois world*. Berkeley: University of California Press.

Darwin, C. 1936a [1859]. *Origin of species by means of natural selection; or, The preservation of favored races in the struggle for life*. New York: Modern Library.

Darwin, C. 1936b [1871]. *The descent of man and selection in relation to sex*. New York: Modern Library.

Davies, A. M. 1987. "Organic" and "organism" in Franz Bopp. In Hoenigswald, H. and L. Wiener (eds) *Biological metaphor and cladistic classification: an interdisciplinary perspective*. Philadelphia: University of Pennsylvania Press. 81–108.

Degraff, M. 2005. Linguistics' most dangerous myth: the fallacy of Creole exceptionalism. *Language in society* 34:533–591.

Derrida, J. 1976. Writing before the Letter. In *Of grammatology*, trans. G. C. Spivak. Baltimore: Johns Hopkins University Press. 3–94.

Dirks, N. 1990. History as a sign of the modern. *Public culture* 2(2):25–32.

Dixon, R. M. W. 1997. *The rise and fall of languages*. New York: Cambridge University Press.

Doke, C. A. 1931. *Report on the unification of the Shona dialects*. Hertford, UK: Stephen Austin and Sons, Ltd.

Donaldson, B. C. 1983. *Dutch – a linguistic history of Holland and Belgium*. Leiden: Martinus Nijhoff.

Eagleton, T. 2000. *The idea of culture*. Malden, MA: Blackwell Publishing.

Endangered Language Fund. n.d. Publicity flyer.

England, N. 1995. Linguistics and indigenous languages: Mayan examples. *Journal of Latin American anthropology* 1(1):122–149.

England, N. 2003. Mayan language revival and revitalization politics. *American anthropologist* 105(4):733–743.

Erdrich, L. 2001. *Last report on the miracles at Little No Horse*. New York: Harper Collins.

Errington, J. 1985. *Language and social change in Java: reflexes of modernization in a traditional royal polity.* Athens, OH: Center for International Studies, Ohio University.

Errington, J. 1988. *Structure and style in Javanese: a semiotic view of linguistic etiquette.* Philadelphia: University of Pennsylvania Press.

Errington, J. 1998. *Shifting languages: interaction and identity in Javanese Indonesia.* New York: Cambridge University Press.

Everett, D. L. 2004. Coherent fieldwork. In van Sterkenberg, P. (ed.) *Linguistics today – facing a greater challenge.* Philadelphia: John Benjamins. 141–162.

Fabian, J. 1983. *Time and the other: how anthropology makes its object.* New York: Columbia University Press.

Fabian, J. 1986. *Language and colonial power: the appropriation of Swahili in the former Belgian Congo 1880–1938.* Berkeley: University of California Press.

Fabri, F. 1859. *Die Entstehung des Heidenthums und die Aufgabe der Heidenmission.* [The origin of heathenry and the task of missions.] Barmen: Langewiesche.

Fabri, F. 1998 [1879]. *Does Germany need colonies?*, trans. E. Breuning and E. Chamberlain. Lewiston, NY: Edwin Mellen Press.

Fanon, F. 1967. *Black skin, white masks*, trans. C. L. Markmann. New York: Grove Press.

Fasold, R. 1984. *The sociolinguistics of society.* Oxford: Blackwell Publishing.

Febvre, L. 1930. *Civilization: evolution of a word and a group of ideas*, vol. 2. Paris: Centre Internationale de Synthèse.

Feld, S. 1996. Waterfalls of song: an acoustemology of place resounding in Bosavi, Papua New Guinea. In Feld, S. and Basso, K. (eds) *Senses of place.* Santa Fe: School of American Research. 91–136.

Ferguson, C. 1959. Diglossia. *Word* 15:325–340.

Fishman, J., Ferguson, C. and Das Gupta, J. (eds) 1968. *Language problems of developing nations.* New York: Wiley and Sons.

Florida, N. K. 1995. *Writing the past, inscribing the future: history as prophecy in colonial Java.* Durham, NC: Duke University Press.

Fokker, A. A. 1891. De waarde van het Maleisch als Beschavingsmedium. [Maly's worth as a cultural language.] *Tijdschrift voor het binnenlandsche bestuur* 5:82–88.

Foucault, M. 1970. *The order of things: an archaeology of the human sciences.* New York: Vintage Books.

Fracchia, J. and Lewontin, R. C. 1999. Does culture evolve? *History and theory* 38:52–70.

French, B. M. 2003. The politics of Mayan linguistics in Guatemala: native speakers, expert analysts, and the nation. *Pragmatics* 13(4):483–498.

Garvin, P. 1954. *Literacy as a problem in language and culture.* Georgetown University Monograph Series on Language and Linguistics No. 7. Washington, DC: Georgetown University Press. 117–129.

Gellner, E. 1983. *Nations and nationalism.* Ithaca: Cornell University Press.

Gellner, E. 1994. Culture, constraint, and community. In *Anthropology and politics.* London: Blackwell Publishing. 45–61

Goody, J. 1986. *The logic of writing and the organization of society.* Cambridge, UK: Cambridge University Press.

Greenblatt, S. 1990. Learning to curse: aspects of linguistic colonialism in the sixteenth century. In *Learning to curse: essays in early modern culture.* Routledge, Chapman and Hall. 16–39.

Greenfeld, L. 1992. *Nationalism: five roads to modernity.* Harvard: Harvard University Press.

Grijns, C. D. 1996. Van der Tuuk and the study of Malay. *Bijdragen tot de Taal-, Land- en Volkenkunde* 152(3):352–381.

Grillo, R. 1989. *Dominant languages: language and hierarchy in Britain and France.* New York: Cambridge University Press.

Grimes, B. (ed.) 1984. *Ethnologue: languages of the world.* Dallas: SIL International.

Grimm, J. 1822. *Deutsche Grammatik.* Göttingen: Dieterischsche Buchhandlung.

Grimm, J. 1984 [1851]. *On the origin of language,* trans. R. A. Wiley. Leiden: Brill.

Groeneboer, K. 1998. *Gateway to the West: the Dutch language in colonial Indonesia 1600–1950.* Amsterdam: Amsterdam University Press.

Gulya, J. 1974. Some eighteenth century antecedents of nineteenth century linguistics: the discovery of Finno-Ugrian. In Hymes, D. (ed.) *Studies in the history of linguistics: traditions and paradigms.* Bloomington: Indian: University Press. 258–276.

Hanke, L. 1937. Pope Paul III and the American Indians. *Harvard theological review* 30:65–102.

Hanke, L. 1949. *The Spanish struggle for justice.* Philadelphia: University of Pennsylvania Press.

Hanks, W. 2000. Genre and textuality. In *Intertexts: writings on language, utterance, and context.* Oxford: Rowman and Littlefield. 103–220.

Harries, P. 1988. The roots of ethnicity: discourse and the politics of language construction in South-east Africa. *African affairs* 87(346):25–52.

Harries, P. 1995. Discovering languages: the historical origins of standard Tsonga in southern Africa. In Mesthrie, R. (ed.) *Language and social history: studies in South African sociolinguistics.* Cape Town: David Philip Publishers. 154–175.

Harris, R. 1980. *The language makers.* London: Duckworth.

Harris, R. 1988. *Language, Saussure, and Wittgenstein: how to play games with words.* London: Routledge.

Hastings, A. 1994. *The Church in Africa, 1450–1950.* Oxford: Oxford University Press.

Heath, S. 1983. *Ways with words: language, life, and work in communities and classrooms.* New York: Cambridge University Press.

Helps, A. 1856–1868. *Spanish conquest in America; and its relation to the history of slavery and to the government of colonies* (4 vols). New York: Harper Brothers.

Henne, M. 1991. Orthographies, language planning, and politics: reflections of an SIL literacy muse. *Notes on literacy* 65:1–18.

Henson, H. 1974. *British social anthropologists and language.* Oxford: Clarendon.

Herder, J. G. 1769. *Kritische Wälder.* [Critical forests.] Riga: Hartnoch.

Herder, J. G. 1966 [1787]. Essay on the origin of language. In *On the origin of language,* trans. J. Moran. New York: F. Ungar. 85–166.

Herzfeld, M. 1987. *Anthropology through the looking-glass: critical ethnography in the margins of Europe.* Cambridge, UK: Cambridge University Press.

Hill, J. 2002. "Expert rhetorics" in advocacy for endangered languages: who is listening, and what do they hear? *Journal of linguistic anthropology* 12(2):119–133.

Hobsbawm, E. 1964. *The age of revolution, 1789–1848.* New York: Mentor.

Hoenigswald, H. 1974. Fallacies in the history of linguistics: notes on the appraisal of the nineteenth century. In Hymes, D. *Studies in the history of linguistics: traditions and paradigms.* Bloomington: Indiana University Press. 346–358.

Hoffman, J. 1973. The Malay language as a force for unity in the Indonesian archipelago. 1815–1900. *Nusantara* 4:19–35.

Hoffman, J. 1979. A foreign investment. *Indonesia* 27:65–92.

Holquist, M. n.d. The roots (home) of exile: Germany. mss.

Hulstaert, G. 1950. *Carte linguistique du Congo Belge.* Mémoires de l'Institut Royal colonial Belge, Vol. XXXVIII, fasc. 1.

von Humboldt, W. 1988 [1836]. *On language: the diversity of human language structure and its influence on the mental development of mankin,* trans. P. Heath. Cambridge, UK: Cambridge University Press.

Illich, I. and Sanders, B. 1988. *The alphabetization of the popular mind.* San Francisco: North Point Press.

International Institute of African Languages and Cultures. 1930. *Practical orthography of African languages.* London: Oxford University Press.

Irschik, E. F. 1969. *Politics and social conflict in South India: the non-Brahman movement and Tamil separatism, 1916–1929.* Berkeley: University of California Press.

Irvine, J. 1993. Mastering African languages: the politics of linguistics in nineteenth century Senegal. In Segal, D. and Handler, R. (eds) *Nations, colonies and metropoles.* Special issue, *Social analysis* 33:27–46.

Irvine, J. 1995. The family romance of colonial linguistics: gender and family in nineteenth century representations of African languages. *Pragmatics* 5(2):139–153.

Irvine, J. 2001. Genres of conquest: from literature to science in colonial African linguistics. In Knoblauch, H. and Kotthoff, H. (eds) *Verbal art across cultures.* Tübingen: Gunter Narr. 63–89.

Irvine, J. and Gal, S. 2000. Language ideology and linguistic differentiation. In Kroskrity, P. (ed.) *Regimes of language: ideologies, polities, and identities.* Santa Fe: School of American Research Press. 35–84.

Jespersen, O. 1894. *Progress in language with special reference to English.* London: Swan Sonnenschien and Co.

Jespersen, O. 1964 [1922]. *Language; its nature, development and origin.* London: G. Allen and Unwin.

Jones, W. 1788. On the orthography of Asiatic words in Roman letters. In *Asiatic researches or, Transactions of the society instituted in Bengal, for inquiring into the history and antiquities, the arts, sciences, and literature of Asia I.* Calcutta: The Society. 1–56.

Joseph, B. D., DeStefano, J., Jacobs, N. G. and Lehiste, I. 2003. *When languages collide: perspectives on language conflict, language competition, and language coexistence.* Columbus: Ohio State University Press. vii–xii.

Joseph, J. 2000. Language and psychological race: Léopold de Saussure on French in Indochina. *Language and communication* 20:29–53.

Joseph, J. 2003. Pictet's *Du Beau* (1856) and the crystallization of Saussurean linguistics. *Historiographia linguistica* 30(3):365–388.

Joseph, J. and Taylor, T. 1990. *Ideologies of language.* New York: Routledge.

Kartunnen, F. 1982. Nahuatl literacy. In Collier, G., Rosaldo, R. and Wirth, J. (eds) *The Inca and Aztec states 1400–1800.* New York: Academic Press. 395–417.

Kiparsky, P. 1974. From paleogrammarians to neogrammarians. In Hymes, D. (ed.) *Studies in the history of linguistics: traditions and paradigms.* Bloomington: Indiana University Press. 331–345.

de Klerk, G. 2002. Mother-tongue education in South Africa: the weight of history. *International journal of the sociology of language* 154:29–46.

Koerner, K. F. 1990. Schlegel and comparative linguistics. In de Mauro, T. and Formigari, L. (eds) *Leibniz, Humboldt, and the origins of comparativism.* Amsterdam: John Benjamins. 239–262.

Krabill, J. R. 1995. *The hymnody of the Harrist Church among the Dida of South-Central Ivory Coast (1913–1949)*. Frankfurt: Peter Lang.

Kroskrity, P. (ed.) 2000. *Regimes of language: ideologies, polities, and identities*. Santa Fe: School of American Research Press.

Ladefoged, P. 1992. Another view of endangered languages. *Language* 68(4):809–811.

Laiou, A. E. 1998. The many faces of medieval colonization. In Boone, E. and Cummins T. (eds) *Native traditions in the postconquest world*. Washington, DC: Dunbarton Oaks. 13–30.

Lehmann, W. 1967. Introduction to a selection from *Deutsche Grammatik*. In *A reader in nineteenth century historical Indo-Europan linguistics*. Bloomington: Indiana University Press. 46–48.

Lepsius, R. 1855. *Standard alphabet for reducing unwritten languages and foreign graphic systems to uniform orthography in European letters*. London: Seeleys.

Levi-Strauss, C. 1967. Linguistics and anthropology. In *Structural anthropology*, trans. C. Jacobson and B. Schoepf. New York: Doubleday. 67–80.

Lewontin, R. 2000. *The triple helix: gene organism, environment*. Harvard: Harvard University Press.

Lockhart, J. 1991. *Nahuas and Spaniards: postconquest Central Mexican history and philology*. Stanford: Stanford University Press.

Lockhart, J. 1992. *Nahuas after the conquest: a social and cultural history of the Indians of Central Mexico, sixteenth through eighteenth centuries*. Stanford: Stanford University Press.

Macaulay, T. B. 1972 [1835]. Minute on Indian education. In Cloive, J. and Pinney, T. (eds) *Selected writings*. Chicago: University of Chicago Press. 237–251.

McClintock, A. 1992. The angel of progress: pitfalls of the term "postcolonialism." *Social text* 31/32:84–98.

McKenzie, D. F. 1985. *Oral culture, literacy and print in early New Zealand: the Treaty of Waitangi*. Wellington: Victoria University Press.

Macormack, S. 1985. The heart has its reasons: predicaments of missionary Christianity in early colonial Peru. *Hispanic American historical review* 65(3):443–466.

Maffi, L. 1999. Language maintenance and revitalization. In Posey, D. (ed.) *Cultural and spiritual values of biodiversity*. Nairobi: United Nations Environment Programme. 37–44.

Maier, H. M. J. 1993. From heteroglossia to polyglossia: the creation of Malay and Dutch in the Indies. *Indonesia* 56:37–65.

Malik, K. 2000. Commentary – let them die. Electronic document, http://wwww.kenanmalik.com/die.htm, accessed May 21, 2006

Mander, J. and Tauli-Corpuz, V. n.d. *Paradigm wars: indigenous peoples' resistance to economic globalization.* San Franciso: International Forum on Globalization.

Mazrui, A. A. 1975. *The political sociology of the English language: an African perspective.* The Hague: Mouton.

Meeuwis, M. 1999. Flemish nationalism in the Belgian Congo versus Zairian anti-imperialism: continuity and discontinuity in language ideological debates. In Blommaert, J. (ed.) *Language ideological debates.* New York: Mouton de Gruyter. 381–424.

Mehnert, W. 1973. The language question in the colonial policy of German imperialism. In *African studies – Afrika studien.* Berlin: Akademi-Verlag-Berlin. 383–398.

Menze, E. and Jenges, K. (eds) 1992. *Herder's selected early works, 1764–1767,* trans. E. Menze and M. Palma. Philadelphia: Pennsylvania State University Press.

Metcalf, G. J. 1974. The Indo-European hypothesis in the sixteenth and seventeenth centuries. In Hymes, D. (ed.) *Studies in the history of linguistics: traditions and paradigms.* Bloomington: Indiana University Press. 233–257.

Meyer, B. 1999. *Translating the devil: religion and modernity among the Ewe in Ghana.* Edinburgh: Edinburgh University Press for the International African Institute.

Mignolo, W. J. 1995. *The darker side of the Renaissance: literacy, territoriality, and colonization.* Ann Arbor: University of Michigan Press.

Miller, J. 2002. How do you say "extinct"?: languages die, the United Nations is upset about this. *Wall Street Journal* March 8:W13.

Mitchell, T. 1988. *Colonising Egypt.* New York: Cambridge University Press.

Mkangi, K. 1985. The political economy of Kiswahili: a Kenya–Tanzania comparison. In Maw, J. and Parkin, D. (eds) *Swahili language and society.* Beiträge zur Afrikanistik, No. 23. Vienna: Institut für Afrikanistik. 331–348.

Muehlebach, A. 2001. Making place at the United Nations: indigenous cultural politics at the U.N. working group on indigenous populations. *Cultural anthropology* 16(3):415–448.

Mufwene, S. 2001. *The ecology of language evolution.* New York: Cambridge University Press.

Mufwene, S. 2003. Language endangerment: what have pride and prestige got to do with it? In Joseph, B. (ed.) *When languages collide: perspectives on language conflict, language competition, and language coexistence.* Columbus: Ohio State University Press. 324–346.

Mühlhaüsler, P. 1996. *Linguistic ecology: language change and linguistic imperialism in the Pacific region*. New York: Routledge.

Müller, M. 1854a. *Proposals for a missionary alphabet*. London: A. and G. Spottiswoode.

Müller, M. 1854b. *Suggestions for the assistance of officers in learning the languages of the seat of war in the East*. London: Longman, Brown, Green, and Longmans.

Nabhan, G. and St. Antoine, S. 1993. The loss of floral and faunal story: the extinction of experience. In Kellert, S. R. and Wilson, E. O. (eds) *The biophilia hypothesis*. Washington, DC: Island Press. 229–250.

de Nebrija, A. 1926 [1492] *Gramática de la lengua castellana*. London: Oxford University Press.

Nietzsche, F. 1979 [1873]. On truth and lies in a nonmoral sense. In *Philosophy and truth. Selections from Nietzsche's notebooks of the early 1870's*, trans. D. Breazeale. Atlantic Highlands, NJ: Humanities Press.

Nietzsche, F. 2004 [1872]. Third lecture on the future of our educational institutions. In *On the future of our educational institution*, trans. and ed. M. Grenke. South Bend, IN: St. Augustine's Press. 61–79.

Niezen, R. 2003. *The origins of indigenism: human rights and the politics of identity*. Berkeley: University of California Press.

Ong, W. J. 1977. *Interfaces of the word: studies in the evolution of consciousness and culture*. Ithaca: Cornell University Press.

van Ophuijsen, C. A. 1910. *Maleische spraakkunst*. Leiden: S.C. van Doesburgh.

Pagden, A. 1982. *The fall of natural man – the American Indian and the origins of comparative ethnology*. New York: Cambridge University Press.

Pagden, A. 1995. The effacement of difference: colonialism and the origins of nationalism in Diderot and Herder. In Prakash, G. (ed.) *After colonialism*. Princeton: Princeton University Press. 129–53.

Pennycook, A. 1998. *English and the discourses of colonialism*. London: Routledge.

Perceval, W. K. 1987. Biological analogy before comparative grammar. In Hoenigswald, H. and Weiner, L. (eds) *Biological metaphor and cladistic classification: an interdisciplinary perspective*. Philadelphia: University of Pennsylvania Press. 3–38.

Perceval, W. K. 1999. Nebrija's linguistic oeuvre as a model for missionary linguists. In Nowak, E. (ed.) *Languages different in all their sounds: descriptive approaches to indigenous languages of the Americas 1500 to 1850*. Studium Sprachwissenschaft Beiheft, No. 31. Munster: Nodus Publikationen. 15–30.

Peterson, D. 2004. *Creative writing: translation, bookkeeping, and the work of imagination in colonial Kenya*. Portsmouth, NH: Heinemann.

Philo, of Alexandria. 1854. *The works of Philo Judaeus, the contemporary of Josephus*, trans. C. D. Yonge. London: H. G. Bohn. Vol. 2.

Pike, K. 1947. *Phonemics: a technique for reducing languages to writing*. Ann Arbor: University of Michigan Press.

Pinker, S. 1995. *The language instinct*. New York: HarperPerennial.

Pollock, S. 2000. Cosmopolitan and vernacular in history. *Public culture* 12(3):591–625.

Powell, R. 2002. Language planning and the British Empire: comparing Pakistan, Malaysia, and Kenya. *Current issues in language planning* 3(3):205–279.

Pramoedya Ananta Toer. 1963. Setelah abad setelah Abdullah Munsji – beberapa aspek historik yang digelapkan. [Half a century after Abdullah Munsji – a few historical aspects which have been hidden.] *Minggu Bintang Timur: Lentera–Lembaran kebudajaan Bintang Timur* [Sunday edition of the Eastern Start, Lantern (culture section)]. August 25, September 22, and October 20.

Pratt, M. L. 1992. *Imperial eyes: travel writing and transculturation*. New York: Routledge.

Pugach, S. 2001. Afrikanistik and colonial knowledge: Carl Meinhof, the missionary impulse and African language and culture studies in Germany, 1887–1919. Ph.D. dissertation, University of Chicago.

Pugach, S. 2004. Carl Meinhof and the German influence on Nicholas van Warmel's ethnological and linguistic writing, 1927–1935. *Journal of Southern African Studies* 30(4):825–845.

Rafael, V. L. 1993. *Contracting colonialism*. Durham, NC: Duke University Press.

Raffles, T. 1979 [1817]. *The history of Java*. Oxford: Oxford University Press.

Raison-Jourde, F. 1977. L'échange inégale de la langue: la pénétration des techniques linguistiques dans une civilisation de l'oral Imerine, début du XIXe siècle. [The unequal exchange of language: the penetration of linguistic techniques in an oral civilization.] *Annales* 32(4):639–669.

Ramaswamy, S. 1993. En/gendering language: the poetics of Tamil identity. *Comparative studies in society and history* 35(4):683–725.

Ranger, T. 1989. Missionaries, migrants and the Manyika: the invention of ethnicity in Zimbabwe. In Vail, L. (ed.) *The creation of tribalism in southern Africa*. Berkeley: University of California Press. 118–150.

Rehg, K. L. 2004. Linguists, literacy, and the law of unintended consequences. *Oceanic linguistics* 43:498–518.

Ricard, R. 1966. *The spiritual conquest of Mexico: an essay on the Apostolate and the evangelizing methods of the Mendicant Orders in New Spain: 1523–1572*, trans. L. Simpson. Berkeley: University of California Press.

Richards, J. 1989. Mayan language planning for bilingual education in Guatemala. *International journal of the sociology of language* 77:93–115.

del Rincón, A. 1885 [1595] *Arte mexicana compuesta por el Padre Anotonia del Rincon de la compañia de Iesus*. Mexico City: Predro Balli.

Rizal, J. 1996 [1887]. *Nole me tangere*, trans. Ma. Soledad Lacson-Locsin, ed. R. L. Locsin. Makati City, Philippines: Bookmark.

Robson, S. O. 1988. *Principles of Indonesian philology*. Providence: Foris Publications.

van Rooden, P. 1996. Nineteenth-century representations of missionary conversion. In van der Veer, P. (ed.) *Conversion to modernities: the globalization of Christianity*. London: Routledge. 65–88.

Rowe, J. R. 1982. Inca policies and institutions relating to the cultural unification of the empire. In Collier, G., Rosaldo, R. and Wirth, J. (eds) *The Inca and Aztec states 1400–1800*. New York: Academic Press. 93–118.

Said, E. 1994. *Orientalism*, 2nd edn. New York: Vintage Books.

Said, E. 1995. Secular interpretation, the geographical element, and the methodology of imperialism. In Prakash, G. (ed.) *After colonialism*. Princeton: Princeton University Press. 21–39.

Samarin, W. J. 1984. The linguistic world of field colonialism. *Language in society* 13:435–453.

de San José, F. 1832 [1610]. *Arte y reglas de la lengua Tagala*. [Grammar of the Tagalog language.] Manila: J. M. Dayot.

Sapir, E. 1949a. *Language: an introduction to the study of speech*. New York: Harcourt Brace.

Sapir, E. 1949b. The psychological reality of the phoneme. In Mandelbaum, D. (ed.) *Selected writings of Edward Sapir*. Berkeley: University of California Press. 46–60.

de Saussure, F. 1966. *Course in general linguistics*, trans. W. Baskin, eds C. Bally and A. Sechehaye. New York: McGraw-Hill.

Schiffman, H. 1996. *Linguistic culture and language policy*. New York: Routledge.

Schlapp, C. 2004. The "genius of language" – transformations of a concept in the history of linguistics. *Historigraphia lingusitica* XXXI(2/3):367–388.

von Schlegel, A. 1965. [1818] *Course of lectures on dramatic art and literature*, trans. J. Black. London: H. G. Bohn.

von Schlegel, F. 1808. *Ueber die Sprache und Weisheit der Indier: Ein Beitrag zur Begrundung der Alterthumskunde*. [The language and wisdom of the Indians.] Heidelberg: Mohr and Zimmer.

Schleicher, A. 1848–50. *Sprachvergleichende Untersuchungen*. [Comparative linguistic reseaches.] Bonn: H. B. König.

Schleicher, A. 1983 [1863]. The Darwinian theory and the science of language. In Koerner, K. (ed.) *Linguistics and evolutionary theory: three essays by August Schleicher, Ernst Haeckel, and Wilhelm Bleek*, trans. A. V. W. Bikkers. Amsterdam: John Benjamins. 1–72.

Schwab, R. 1984. *Oriental renaissance*, trans. G. Patterson-Black and V. Reinking. New York: Columbia University Press.

Scott, W. H. 1994. *Barangay: sixteenth century Philippine culture and society*. Manila: Ateneo de Manila University Press.

Seed, P. 1991. "Failing to marvel": Atahualpa's encounter with the word. *Latin American reseach review* 26(1):7–32.

Seitz, G. 1984. *Die Bruder Grimm: Leben–Werk–Zeit*. Munich: Winkler.

Silverstein, M. 1996. Monoglot "standard" in America: standardization and metaphors of linguistic hegemony. In Brenneis, D. and Macaulay, R. K. S. (eds) *The matrix of language: contemporary linguistic anthropology*. Boulder: Westview Press. 284–306.

Skutnabb-Kangas, T. 1999. Linguistic diversity and language rights. In Posey, D. (ed.) *Cultural and spiritual values of biodiversity*. Nairobi: United Nations Environment Programme. 46–54.

Smalley, W. A. 1958. Respect and ethnocentrism. *Practical anthropology* 5:191–194.

Smith, C. C. 1999. The vernacular. In McKitterick, R. (ed.) *The New Cambridge Medieval History*, vol. 5. Cambridge: Cambridge University Press. 71–83.

Smith, V. A. 1919. *The Oxford history of India, from the earliest times to the end of 1911*, 3rd edn. Oxford: Clarendon Press.

Sneddon, J. 2003. *The Indonesia language: its history and role in modern society*. Sydney: University of New South Wales Press.

Steiner, P. 1975. *After Babel: aspects of language and translation*. Oxford: Oxford University Press.

Steinmetz, G. 2003. "The devil's handwriting": precolonial discourse, ethnographic acuity and cross-identification in German colonialism. *Comparative studies in society and history* 45(1):41–95.

Stoler, A. L. 1985. *Capitalism and confrontation in Sumatra's plantation belt 1870–1979*. New Haven: Yale University Press.

Stoler, A. 2002. *Carnal knowledge and imperial power: race and the intimate in colonial rule*. Berkeley: University of California Press.

Stoll, D. 1982. *Fishers of men or founders of empire? The Wycliffe Bible translators in Latin America*. London: Zed Press.

Street, B. 1984. *Literacy in theory and practice*. New York: Cambridge University Press.

Stumpf, R. 1979. *La politique linguistique au Cameroun de 1884 à 1960: comparaison entre les administrations coloniales allemande, francaise et britannique et du rôle joué par les sociétés missionaires*. [Linguistic politics in Cameroon

1884–1960: a comparison of the German, French, and British colonial administrations, and the roles of the missionary societies.] Berne: Peter Lang.

Sutherland, W. 2003. Parallel extinction risk and global distribution of languages and species. *Nature* 423(May 15):276–279.

Sylvain, R. 2002. Land, water, and truth: San identity and global indigenism. *American anthropologist* 104(4):1074–1086.

Tavárez, D. 2000. Naming the Trinity: from ideologies of translation to dialectics of reception in colonial Nahua texts, 1547–1771. *Colonial Latin American review* 9(1):21–47.

Taylor, C. 1995. The importance of Herder. In *Philosophical arguments*. Harvard: Harvard University Press. 79–99.

Taylor, C. 2002. Modern social imaginaries. *Public culture* 14(1):91–124.

Taylor, C. 2004. *Modern social imaginaries*. Durham, NC: Duke University Press.

Taylor, J. 1983. *The social world of Batavia: European and Eurasian in Dutch Asia*. Madison: University of Wisconsin Press.

Tedlock, D. 1983. *The spoken word and the work of interpretation*. Philadelphia: University of Pennsylvania Press.

Teeuw, A. 1971. Introduction. In van der Tuuk, H. *A grammar of Toba Batak*, trans. J. Scott-Kemball. KITLV Translation Series No. 13. The Hague: Martinus Nijhoff. xiii–xxxix.

Teeuw, A. 1973. *Pegawai bahasa dan ilmu bahasa*, trans. J. M. Polak. [Language officers and Indonesian linguistics.] Jakarta: Bhratara Publishers.

Thoreau, H. D. 1962. *The journal of Henry D. Thoreau*, ed. B. Torrey and F. Allen. 14 vols. New York: Dover.

Thorne, S. 1999. *Congregational missions and the making of an imperial culture in nineteenth-century England*. Stanford: Stanford University Press.

Todorov, T. 1984. *The conquest of America: the question of the other*, trans. R. Howard. New York: Harper and Row.

Topping, D. 2003. Saviors of language: who will be the real Messiah? *Oceanic linguistics* 42:522–527.

Trautmann, T. R. 1997. *Aryans and British India*. Berkeley: University of California Press.

Trautmann, T. R. 2006. *Languages and nations: the Dravidian proof in colonial Madras*. Berkeley: University of California Press.

Trend, J. B. 1944. *The civilization of Spain*. London: Oxford University Press.

van der Tuuk, H. 1962. *De pen in gal gedoopt. Brieven en documenten verzameld en toegelicht door R. Nieuwenhuys*. [With a pen dipped in bile. Letters and documents assembled with an introduction by R. Nieuwenhuys.] Amsterdam: G. A. van Oorschot.

van der Tuuk, H. 1971 [1864, 1867] *A grammar of Toba Batak*, trans. J. Scott-Kemball. KITLV Translation Series No. 13. The Hague: Martinus Nijhoff.

Vail, L. (ed.) 1989. *The creation of tribalism in southern Africa*. Berkeley: University of California Press.

Valentijn, F. 1724–26. *Oude en nieuw Oost-Indiën: vervattende een naauwkeurige en uitvoerige verhandelinghe van Nederlands mogentheyd in die gewesten*, 5 vols. [Old and new East Indies: containing a careful and detailed essay on the Netherlands' power in the west.] Amsterdam: Van Braam, Onder de Linden.

Valla, L. 1488 [1441] *Elegantiae linguae Latinae*. Venice: Bartholomaeus de Zanis.

van der Veer, P. 2001. *Imperial encounters: religion and modernity in India and Britain*. Princeton: Princeton University Press.

Van der Velde, M. 1999. The two language maps of the Belgian Congo. *Annales aequatoria* 20:475–489.

Vikor, L. 1988. *Perfecting spelling: spelling discussions and reforms in Indonesia and Malaysia*. Dordrecht: Foris Publications.

Wallis, E. and Bennett, M. 1959. *Two thousand tongues to go: the story of the Wycliffe Bible translators*. New York: Harper and Bros.

Warneck, G. 1901. *Outline of a history of Protestant missions*, ed. G. Robson. New York: Fleming Revell.

Warren, K. 1998. *Indigenous movements and their critics: pan-Maya activism in Guatemala*. Princeton: Princeton University Press.

Weber, E. 1976. *Peasants into Frenchmen: the modernization of rural France, 1870–1914*. Stanford: Stanford University Press.

Werndly, G. H. 1736. *Maleische spraakkunst. Uit de eige schriften der Maleiers opgemaakt*. [Malay grammar, from the Malays' own script.] Amsterdam: Wetstein.

Whitney, W. D. 1873. Dr. Bleek and the simious theory of language. In *Oriental and linguistic studies: the Veda; the Avesta; the science of language*. New York: Scribner, Armstrong and Co. 292–297.

Wittgenstein, L. 1953. *Philosophical investigations*, ed. G. E. M. Anscombe. New York: Macmillan Co.

Woolf, L. 1919. *Empire and commerce in Africa: a study in economic imperialism*. London: Allen and Unwin.

Wright, R. 2003. *Sociophilological study of late Latin*. Turnhout: Brepols.

Zammito, J. H. 2002. *Kant, Herder and the birth of anthropology*. Chicago: University of Chicago Press.

Zipes, J. 1988. *The brothers Grimm: from enchanted forests to the modern world*. New York: Routledge.

Languages Index

Persons Index

Subject Index

CPSIA information can be obtained
at www.ICGtesting.com
Printed in the USA
BVHW091532170722
641988BV00007B/160

9 781405 105705